AN ACCESS GUIDE FOR SCRIPTURE STUDY

The Gospel According to John

Peter Francis Ellis, S.S.L.
and
Judith Monahan Ellis

William H. Sadlier, Inc.
New York   Chicago   Los Angeles

Nihil Obstat:
John P. Meier, S.S.D.
Censor Librorum

Imprimatur:
Joseph T. O'Keefe, D.D.
Vicar General
Archdiocese of New York
November 3, 1982

The *Nihil Obstat* and *Imprimatur* are official declarations that a book or pamphlet is free of doctrinal or moral error. No implication is contained therein that those who have granted the *Nihil Obstat* and *Imprimatur* agree with the contents, opinions, or statements expressed.

Library of Congress Catalog Card Number: 82-061455
International Standard Book Number: 0-8215-5918-4
 23456789/98765

Published by
William H. Sadlier, Inc.
11 Park Place
New York, New York 10007

Printed and bound in the United States of America

The text of the Gospel of John and all excerpts from Scripture are from the *Good News Bible*, the Bible in Today's English Version. Copyright © American Bible Society, 1976.

Contents

For Judy's parents,
Wilfred and Viola Monahan

"Easy access to sacred Scripture should be provided for all the Christian faithful."

Dogmatic Constitution on Divine Revelation, Vatican II

Preface

The study of Scripture is among the oldest and most traditional religious activities in our Christian heritage. The Gospel of Mark and the Gospel of Luke begin their account of Jesus' public ministry by telling us that he read and preached on the Scriptures in the synagogue in Galilee. It was through their knowledge of the Scriptures that Jesus explained the meaning of his death and resurrection to the two disciples on the way to Emmaus. Readings from the Scriptures have been part of our liturgies since the time of the apostles.

Since the Scriptures are not contemporary works, today's audience needs some guidance to understand fully what the authors are trying to communicate to us about the faith of their communities and the events that generated that great faith. Like most carefully written and thoughtful literature, the books of the Bible have depths of meaning not always apparent to the casual reader. Experience tells us that clear guidance and attentive study can be the key to deeper understanding that will lead to rewarding reflection and prayer.

The *Access Guide* series is designed to help beginning and experienced readers of the sacred Scriptures arrive at a better understanding of the books of the

Bible and a familiarity with their role in the development of faith. Each book has been written by a noted authority on that particular part of the Bible. The language is clear, and the text is presented in a highly readable manner.

The general introduction of each study guide acquaints the reader with the background of the particular book of the Bible being studied. It provides information about the biblical author, the historical period in which the book was written, and the nature of the community that was the first audience for the book. The theological themes which summarize the author's message are also discussed, giving the reader an idea of what to look for in considering each section of the book.

A thumbnail sketch of each book of the Bible provides the reader with a basic outline that indicates how the author organized his account of the events in order better to communicate his message. It is interesting to note that, in their original form, the books of the Bible were not divided into chapters and verses. Most had no punctuation or even spaces between the words. The organization of the text, as we know it today, took place at a much later date. Often this organization was done by scholars who failed to appreciate the original organization of the authors' thoughts. The sections of the books are organized in these guides in such a way as to reflect the natural internal flow of the original authors' manuscripts.

Likewise, since the ancient Hebrew, Greek, and Aramaic languages are no longer commonly spoken, there are many variations in the way the Scriptures are translated into English. The preferred translation for this series is the *Good News Bible* because of its readability in contemporary English. The reader may choose another translation or wish to compare translations which vary. Certainly, recognizing differences in the interpretation of the Scriptures will enhance the reader's ability to get more out of each passage.

The *Access Guide* series is designed for both group and individual study. All the information needed to use the study guides is provided. Groups, however, may wish to have a discussion leader and use the edition of the *Access Guide* which contains notes for the discussion leader. Individual readers and group participants are encouraged to have a complete Bible on hand for reference purposes.

The material in each study guide is arranged into six study sessions. This format will help those in discussion groups plan each session around a specific sequence of the Scripture text and give some direction to the discussions. A group leader may find it more convenient to rearrange the material into a greater or fewer number of sessions.

Each of the six study sessions contains a portion of Scripture and commentary. Questions for discussion and reflection are meant to lead the reader to probe more deeply into the significance of the Scripture for its first audience and for the contemporary Christian. Naturally, a renewed understanding of the Scriptures and a fresh discovery of the riches contained therein will lead to reflection and prayer and be shared with others through discussion and celebration.

General Introduction to John, the Fourth Gospel

The Purpose of the Writer and the Nature of the Community

John says that he wrote his Gospel "in order that you may believe that Jesus is the Messiah, the Son of God, and that through your faith in him you may have life" (20:31). These words, however, tell only half the story of why John wrote his Gospel. Other parts of his Gospel (for example, 9:20–23, 12:37–43) indicate that he wrote for a rather special audience, namely for Jewish Christians on the fence between Judaism and Christianity, unable to give up the security of the synagogue and commit themselves fully to the persecuted Christian Church.

John's audience was Jewish—Jewish Christians who had spent their lives worshiping in the synagogue. They believed in Jesus and Christianity but continued to belong to the synagogue, rightly seeing Christianity as the fulfillment of the Old Testament and themselves as true Israelites now called by God to believe in Jesus.

The leaders of the synagogue, however, did not see things the same way. To begin with, they did not believe in Jesus; nor did they intend to put up with Jews who did. As a consequence, in the last decades of the first century, when John wrote his Gospel, the synagogue leaders had begun to persecute Jewish Christians in order to compel them to abandon Christianity and return to the faith of their ancestors. Christian Jews were given the grim choice of either repudiating Jesus or turning away from the synagogue. Those who decided for Jesus and Christianity were expelled from the synagogue, scorned as heretics, deprived of privileges in the community, and in general treated as outcasts.

Not content with expelling Jewish Christians, the synagogue leaders launched a propaganda campaign against Jesus and the Christians. They contended that since Christians worshiped Jesus as God and Yahweh as God, they were worshiping two gods. Thus, they accused Jewish Christians of giving up the most sacred belief of Judaism, namely, the belief that there is only one God. In addition, the synagogue leaders derided the Christians' belief that Jesus was the promised Messiah and that in the Eucharist they partook of Jesus' body and blood.

Between the persecutions and the propaganda, Jewish Christians were having a difficult time. Some found the situation too much for them and began to reconsider their conversion to Christianity. John wrote his Gospel to dispel their doubts and to strengthen their resolve to get off the fence once and for all and to put their faith entirely in Jesus, whatever the consequences. To accomplish this purpose, John felt he had to do at least three things. First, he had to present clearly in his Gospel what Christians believed about Jesus and especially what they believed about his divinity. Second, he had to make it clear that genuine Christian faith rested not on belief in Jesus' miracles but on belief in Jesus himself. Third, he had to refute the damaging accusations made by the synagogue leaders against Jesus and Christianity.

Major Theological Themes

John's central theological themes deal with the person of Jesus—his divinity, his purpose in becoming man, and the response of faith he calls for from Christians in the world. Like Matthew, Mark, and Luke, John professes his belief in Jesus as the Son of God, as the Messiah, and as the one who fulfills all that the Old Testament predicted of him as the Messiah. However, John has a unique way of expressing his major theological themes. He puts them all under the key word "work." He declares that **the work of the Father** is to give his own Son Jesus, out of love, unto death for the salvation of the world (John's theology); **the work of Jesus** is to do the will of the Father by dying on the cross, thereby both showing his love for the world and bringing the world to believe in him (John's Christology); **the work of the world** is to respond to the love of the Father and the Son by believing in the Son and by giving themselves out of love one for another as Jesus gave himself out of love for them (John's theology of discipleship).

Literary Techniques

Literary techniques are devices used by writers of all ages to put across their message. John's techniques are used both in ancient and modern literature, but they need to be pointed out to modern readers who usually do not expect to find them in an inspired Gospel. John uses such literary techniques as **double-meaning words**, that is, words which have one meaning for the speaker and another for the person addressed (for example, in 4:10–14, where the Samaritan woman is thinking of ordinary water and Jesus means the water of eternal life). He also uses the **misunderstanding** technique whereby someone is made to grossly misunderstand Jesus. This technique allows John to give Jesus the opportunity to explain himself more fully and thus to explain his (John's) theology (for example, 2:19–22; 3:3–8; 4:7–14). **Irony** is another technique. Here statements have one meaning for the speaker who thinks he speaks the truth and another meaning for the author and the reader who know the truth to be quite the opposite (for example, 4:12; 7:42; 11:49–50; 18:38).

John also uses **explanatory comments**. These comments are like footnotes and are used to explain and sometimes to correct the readers' impressions (for example, 2:21–22; 3:24; 4:2; 6:6). Finally, John uses **discourses** as a literary technique. His discourses usually begin with a mysterious statement by Jesus, followed by a question or a misunderstanding which is then clarified by Jesus' subsequent discourse (for example 3:1–21; 4:10–26).

The Place of John in the New Testament

Anyone who reads the Gospels notices that Matthew, Mark, and Luke give a great deal of space to the story of **what** Jesus did. They give long accounts of Jesus' birth, his travels, his encounters with friends and enemies, his parables, his miracles, and especially his passion, death, and resurrection. In John's Gospel, on the other hand, the reader notices almost immediately that John concentrates much more on **who** Jesus is rather than on **what** Jesus does. The reader has no doubt that John is talking about the same person as the synoptic writers, that he has the same belief in Jesus, and that he follows the same basic outline of Jesus' life. Yet John has no account of Jesus' birth, says little about Jesus' miracles (he records only seven), and mentions not a single parable told by Matthew, Mark, and Luke. John presupposes his readers know all these things. He concentrates his energies, therefore, on the person of Jesus and on persuading Jewish Christians to get off the fence and decide for Jesus. It is for this reason that he fills his Gospel with discourses and dialogues dealing with who Jesus is and why it is necessary to have faith in him in order to attain eternal life.

John's place in the New Testament is that of the theologian of the Trinity. He goes beneath the surface meaning of what Jesus said and did. He attempts to explain the deeper meaning of Jesus' divine person, the relationship of Jesus to the Father and to the Holy Spirit, and the critical importance of Jesus for the salvation of the world. In symbolic descriptions of the evangelists, John is represented by an eagle. He is the theologian who soars into the heart of the Trinity to discover and proclaim the depth of the love that unites Father, Son, and Holy Spirit and overflows abundantly upon all humankind.

A Thumbnail
Sketch
of John

This study guide begins with an outline showing the carefully worked out structure of John's Gospel. To appreciate the structure of this Gospel, the reader should remember that John follows Middle Eastern rather than Western norms for literary art. Principal among these norms is the Middle Eastern fondness for symmetry and parallelism. The following diagram with its twenty-one symmetrical sequences is included here to help the reader appreciate both the skill and the care with which John structured his Gospel as a whole.

It is immediately evident that the themes of sequence 21 (20:19—21:25) parallel and mirror back the themes of sequence 1 (1:19–51); sequence 20 (20:1–18), those of sequence 2 (2:1–12); sequence 19 (18:1—19:42), those of sequence 3 (2:13–25); and so on. The pattern provides the reader with an easy way to memorize the key sequences of the Gospel. Structuring John's Gospel thus, in sequences, proves to be a very effective tool for reemphasizing, by means of repetition, the key truths John wanted to impress upon his readers.

Sequence 11 (6:16–21), which is at top center of this parallel staircase structure (if we may call it that), is the hinge or turning point of John's Gospel. It is around this sequence, that all of John's theology revolves.

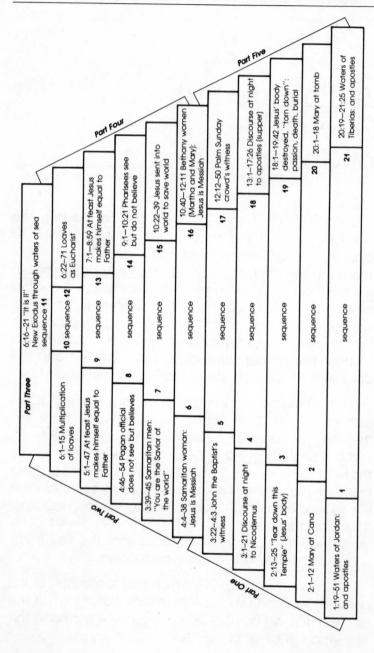

Part Three

6:16–21 "It is I!"
New Exodus through waters of sea
11 sequence 10

6:22–71 Loaves
as Eucharist
12 sequence

7:1–8:59 At feast Jesus
makes himself equal to
Father
13 sequence

9:1–10:21 Pharisees see
but do not believe
14 sequence

10:22–39 Jesus sent into
world to save world
15 sequence

10:40–12:11 Bethany women
(Martha and Mary):
Jesus is Messiah
16 sequence

12:12–50 Palm Sunday
crowd's witness
17 sequence

13:1–17:26 Discourse at night
to apostles (supper)
18 sequence

18:1–19:42 Jesus' body
destroyed, "torn down":
passion, death, burial
19 sequence

20:1–18 Mary at tomb
20 sequence

20:19–21:25 Waters of
Tiberias: and apostles
21

Part Four

Part Five

6:1–15 Multiplication
of loaves
10 sequence **12**

5:1–47 At feast Jesus
makes himself equal to
Father
9 sequence **13**

4:46–54 Pagan official
does not see but believes
8 sequence **14**

3:39–45 Samaritan men:
"You are the Savior of
the world"
7 sequence **15**

4:4–38 Samaritan woman:
Jesus is Messiah
6 sequence **16**

3:22–4:3 John the Baptist's
witness
5 sequence **17**

3:1–21 Discourse at night
to Nicodemus
4 sequence **18**

2:13–25 "Tear down this
Temple" (Jesus' body)
3 sequence **19**

2:1–12 Mary at Cana
2 sequence

1:19–51 Waters of Jordan:
and apostles
1 sequence

Part Two

Part One

First, however, we must note John's overall outline of his Gospel. The Gospel as a whole has five major parts:

Part One 1:1—4:3	Presentation of Jesus' credentials (prologue and sequences 1–5).
Part Two 4:4—6:15	Positive and negative responses to Jesus (sequences 6–10).
Part Three 6:16–21	Hinge or turning point of the Gospel in which Jesus, like Yahweh, leads his people across the sea to a new life (sequence 11).
Part Four 6:22—12:11	Refutation of accusations against Jesus (sequences 12–16).
Part Five 12:12—21:25	Last days of Jesus: his entry into Jerusalem, Last Supper discourse, passion, death, and resurrection (sequences 17–21).

This study of John's Gospel will deal with Part One (1:1—4:3) in study session one; Parts Two (4:4—6:15) and Three (6:16–21) in study session two. Study sessions three and four will deal with the long Part Four (6:22—12:11) and study sessions five and six will deal with the even longer Part Five (12:12—21:25).

Part One Jesus' Credentials ——— John 1:1—4:3

John structured his Gospel, as we have just seen, in the form of an up-and-down parallel staircase. By means of this structure he is able to repeat and thus reemphasize all the dominant themes of his Gospel. Beginning with Part One (1:1—4:3), he uses this same staircase structure in each of the five parts of his Gospel. As shown in the chart on page 16, each part (except Part Three) has five sequences, of which the fifth mirrors back the first, and the fourth mirrors back the second, with the third as the hinge of each part, just as sequence 11 (6:16–21) is the hinge of the entire five-part Gospel structure.

The Gospel begins with John's prologue (1:1–18) and continues with the following five sequences of Part One:

1—John the Baptist and others witness to Jesus (1:19–51).
2—Jesus changes water into wine at Cana (2:1–12).
3—Jesus "replaces" the Old Temple (2:13–25).
4—Jesus speaks to Nicodemus about rebirth through water and the Holy Spirit (3:1–21).
5—John the Baptist again witnesses to Jesus (3:22–4:3).

John has carefully delineated each sequence. The first takes place at the Jordan with John the Baptist; the second at Cana; the third in Jerusalem; the fourth at night with Nicodemus; and the fifth returns again to the Baptist. Part One begins with the prologue and then deals with the message of each successive sequence. Along the way, the reader will see the relationship of one sequence to another and the interrelationship of all five sequences around a common theme.

The Prologue (1:1—18)

John's prologue describes in majestic Semitic prose the descending-ascending movement of the Second Person of the Blessed Trinity from heaven to earth and back again to heaven. It is called a prologue because it precedes and sums up in deeply theological declarations the central themes of the Gospel. It could also be called a preface because it does what a preface is supposed to do: it provides an introduction to the Gospel as a whole. Whether we call this beginning of John his prologue or his preface, it was specially written by the evangelist both to introduce his Gospel and at the same time provide for his readers a summary of his theological themes.

Throughout the Gospel, the reader will notice that each sequence has been divided into five paragraphs. This has been done because scholars have noticed that John parallels paragraph one with paragraph five, and paragraph two with paragraph four. The reader who compares these parallel paragraphs will notice similarities either in words, or expression, or content. John parallels his paragraphs to help his readers remember each sequence more easily.

The Gospel According to John

Prologue (1:1–18)

1 Before the world was created, the Word already existed; he was with God, and he was the same as God. ²From the very beginning, the Word was with God. ³Through him God made all things; not one thing in all creation was made without him. ⁴The Word had life in himself, and this life brought light to men. ⁵The light shines in the darkness, and the darkness has never put it out. ⁶God sent his messenger, a man named John, ⁷who came to tell people about the light. He came to tell them, so that all should hear the message and believe. ⁸He himself was not the light; he came to tell about the light.

⁹This was the real light, the light that comes into the world and shines on all men. ¹⁰The Word, then, was in the world. God made the world through him, yet the world did not know him. ¹¹He came to his own country, but his own people did not receive him.

¹²Some, however, did receive him and believed in him; so he gave them the right to become God's children. ¹³They did not become God's children by natural means, by being born as the children of a human father; God himself was their Father.

¹⁴The Word became a human being and lived among us. We saw his glory, full of grace and truth. This was the glory which he received as the Father's only Son.

¹⁵John told about him. He cried out, "This is the one I was talking about when I said, 'He

comes after me, but he is greater than I am, because he existed before I was born' " ¹⁶Out of the fullness of his grace he has blessed us all, giving us one blessing after another. ¹⁷God gave the Law through Moses; but grace and truth came through Jesus Christ. ¹⁸No one has ever seen God. The only One, who is the same as God and is at the Father's side, he has made him known.

The prologue begins with the central theme of the Gospel, the divinity of Jesus: "Before the world was created, . . . he was the same as God" (1:1). The theme of Jesus' divine nature will be developed in Jesus' discourse to the Jews following his cure of the paralytic in 5:1—47, in Jesus' discourse at the Festival of Shelters in 7:1—8:59, and in Jesus' discourse at the Festival of the Dedication in 10:22–39. It is further asserted in the prologue that the Word took part with the Father in the creation of the world and all that is in it (1:1). This theme is taken up only in a very indirect way in 2:1–13 in the story of the creating of wine out of water; and in 5:17–30, in which Jesus speaks of working as the Father works. The theme of 1:4, "The Word was the source of life, and this life brought light to mankind," runs throughout the Gospel. That Jesus is "the source of life" is the main theme of his night discourse to Nicodemus (3:1–21), his discourse to the Samaritan woman (4:4–38), and his discourse to the Jews about the bread from heaven (6:22–71).

The theme of 1:5, "The light shines in the darkness, and the darkness has never put it out," is especially prominent in the night discourse to Nicodemus (3:1–21), where Jesus speaks about those who come to the light as opposed to those who love the darkness and stay away from the light. In 8:12, Jesus explicitly declares, "I am the light of the world." Throughout the Gospel, Jesus' enemies (the "darkness") try to destroy him, but their efforts result only in the light's shining all the brighter after Jesus' resurrection from the dead.

The Baptist's witness to Jesus in 1:6–9 is given both at the beginning of Part One when Jesus comes to the Baptist at the Jordan (1:19–34) and at the end of Part One of the Gospel when the Baptist's disciples complain that more people are following Jesus than are following the Baptist (3:22–4:3). As we will see, the evangelist considers the Baptist's testimony of the highest importance.

In 1:10–11, John speaks about the world's response to Jesus. Even though Jesus comes to enlighten the whole world, not everyone is willing to listen and be enlightened. The Samaritan woman (4:4–38), the Samaritan townspeople (4:39–45), and the government official (4:46–54) are willing to listen, and they are enlightened and brought to believe in Jesus. But when Jesus cures the paralytic in Jerusalem (5:1–47), the Jerusalem Jews neither listen nor believe. And when he feeds five thousand with five loaves in Galilee (6:1–15), the Galilean Jews neither listen nor understand.

In 1:12–13, John describes those who respond positively to Jesus, who believe in him, and as a result become the children of God, born through God's gift of faith which they accept with open minds and grateful hearts. In the Gospel they are represented by all those who remain united to Jesus, "the real vine," and as a consequence produce much fruit (15:1–17). John's great Last Supper discourse (13:1–17:26) is directed in its entirety to those who have become the children of God, that is, to all of Jesus' disciples down through the centuries.

The words of 1:14 are momentous: "The Word became a human being and, full of grace and truth, lived among us." They encapsulate the second major theme of the Gospel, namely, the incarnation of the Second Person of the Blessed Trinity and his living amongst us in the flesh.

The end of the prologue (1:15–18) repeats through the words of the Baptist ("he existed before I was born") the truth of Jesus' preexistence, earlier expressed in 1:1: "Before the world was created, the Word already existed."

"Out of the fullness of his grace" (1:16) describes the riches of the new covenant. This description is continued (1:17) by contrasting what God gave through Moses (the law—the revelation contained in the Old Testament) with what he has given through Jesus—"grace and truth."

The prologue ends (1:18) as it began with a reference to God the Father and his Son Jesus, now returned to the place where he was before his incarnation as man—"at the Father's side."

■ *Reflection*

Think about key words (such as, "life," "light," "grace," "truth") in the prologue of John's Gospel and what they should mean to one who receives and believes in Jesus.

Sequence 1 (1:19–51)
Witnesses to Jesus

In this sequence (1:19–51) John uses a parade of witnesses both to exemplify and to dramatize what he means by believing in Jesus. The parade begins with John the Baptist, continues with Andrew, Philip, and Nathanael, and ends with Jesus himself.

Sequence 1 (1:19–51)

[19] This is what John said when the Jews in Jerusalem sent priests and Levites to ask him, "Who are you?" [20] John did not refuse to answer, but declared openly and clearly, "I am not the Messiah." [21] "Who are you, then?" they asked. "Are you Elijah?" "No, I am not," John answered. "Are you the Prophet?" they asked. "No," he replied. [22] "Tell us who you are," they said. "We have to take an answer back to those who sent us. What do you say about yourself?" [23] John answered, "This is what I am: 'The voice of one who shouts in the desert: Make a straight path for the Lord to travel!' " (This is what the prophet Isaiah had said.) [24] The messengers had been sent by the Pharisees. [25] They asked John, "If you are not the Messiah, nor Elijah, nor the Prophet, why do you baptize?" [26] John answered: "I baptize with water; among you stands the one you do not know. [27] He comes after me, but I am not good enough even to untie his sandals." [28] All this happened in Bethany, on the other side of the Jordan river, where John was baptizing. [29] The next day John saw Jesus coming to him and said: "Here is the Lamb of God who takes away the sin of the world! [30] This is the one I was talking about when I said, 'A man comes after me, but he is greater than I am, because he existed before I was born.' [31] I did not know who he would be, but I came baptizing with water in order to make him known to Israel." [32] This is the testimony that John gave: "I saw the Spirit come down like a dove from heaven and stay on him. [33] I still did not know him, but God, who sent me to baptize with water, said to me, 'You will see the Spirit come down and stay on a man; he is the one who baptizes with the Holy Spirit.' [34] I have seen it," said John, "and I tell

you that he is the Son of God." ³⁵The next day John was there again with two of his disciples, ³⁶when he saw Jesus walking by. "Here is the Lamb of God!" he said. ³⁷The two disciples heard him say this and went with Jesus. ³⁸Jesus turned, saw them following him, and asked, "What are you looking for?" They answered, "Where do you live, Rabbi?" (This word, translated, means "Teacher.") ³⁹"Come and see," he answered. So they went with him and saw where he lived, and spent the rest of that day with him. (It was about four o'clock in the afternoon.)

⁴⁰One of the two who heard John, and went with Jesus, was Andrew, Simon Peter's brother. ⁴¹At once Andrew found his brother Simon and told him, "We have found the Messiah." (This word means "Christ.")

⁴²Then he brought Simon to Jesus. Jesus looked at him and said, "You are Simon, the son of John. Your name will be Cephas." (This is the same as Peter, and means "Rock.")

⁴³The next day Jesus decided to go to Galilee. He found Philip and said to him, "Come with me!" (⁴⁴Philip was from Bethsaida, the town where Andrew and Peter lived.) ⁴⁵So Philip found Nathanael and told him: "We have found the one of whom Moses wrote in the book of the Law, and of whom the prophets also wrote. He is Jesus, the son of Joseph, from Nazareth."

⁴⁶"Can anything good come from Nazareth?" Nathanael asked. "Come and see," answered Philip. ⁴⁷When Jesus saw Nathanael coming to him, he said about him, "Here is a real Israelite; there is nothing false in him!" ⁴⁸Nathanael asked him, "How do you know

me?" Jesus answered, "I saw you when you were under the fig tree, before Philip called you." [49]"Teacher," answered Nathanael, "you are the Son of God! You are the King of Israel!" [50]Jesus said, "Do you believe just because I told you I saw you when you were under the fig tree? You will see much greater things than this!" [51]And he said to them, "I tell you the truth: you will see heaven open and God's angels going up and coming down on the Son of Man!"

When the Jewish authorities ask the Baptist, "Who are you?" he replies without hesitation that he himself is not the Messiah, but only the herald of the Messiah who comes after him and whose sandals he is not "good enough even to untie" (1:19–27).

When the Baptist sees Jesus coming toward him, he declares forthrightly, "There is the Lamb of God, who takes away the sin of the world!" (1:29). His words are a summary of the whole work of redemption. At the end of the Gospel, the evangelist will show that Jesus dies as the "lamb" of the new and eternal Passover, thus taking away the sin of the world and reconciling all humankind to God.

The Baptist's witness continues with his declarations that Jesus "existed before [he] was born" (1:30), that he "saw the Spirit come down like a dove from heaven and stay on him" (1:32), and that Jesus "is the Son of God" (1:34).

After the Baptist, it is the first disciples' turn to give witness. Andrew tells Peter, "We have found the Messiah" (1:41). Philip tells Nathanael, "We have found the one whom Moses wrote about in the book of the Law and whom the prophets also wrote about" (1:45).

Nathanael speaks to Jesus and says, "Teacher, . . . you are the son of God! You are the King of Israel!" (1:49). Finally, Jesus testifies to himself by saying to Nathanael, "Do you believe just because I told you I saw you under the fig tree? You will see much greater things than this! . . . I am telling you the truth: you will see heaven open and God's angels going up and coming down on the Son of Man" (1:51).

The parade of witnesses here in sequence 1 and the heaping up of titles, for example, Lamb of God, the preexistent one, the Son of God, the Messiah, the one about whom Moses and the prophets wrote, the King of Israel, and the Son of Man, constitute for all practical purposes a summary of what the evangelist and the members of his Christian community believed about Jesus at the end of the first century. These beliefs, of course, will be expressed more fully and more clearly in the body of the Gospel. What John has done, admittedly in an artificial manner, here in the opening sequence of his Gospel, is to render massive theological witness to the person of Jesus. Christian audiences would unhesitatingly say "Amen" to this witness. Other persons would unhesitatingly deny it. And still others would say, "Would that we could believe it!" It is for these last that John wrote his Gospel as he tells us in 20:31: "But these [miracles] have been written in order that you may believe that Jesus is the Messiah, the Son of God, and that through your faith in him you may have life."

Sequence 2 (2:1–12)
Mary at Cana

On paper, credentials can be impressive, but they are worthless if not verified in fact. John, therefore, first testifies to who Jesus is (the divine Messiah in 1:1–51) and then in this sequence shows how Jesus verifies his credentials.

Sequence 2 (2:1–12)

2 Two days later there was a wedding in the town of Cana, in Galilee. Jesus' mother was there, ²and Jesus and his disciples had also been invited to the wedding.

³When all the wine had been drunk, Jesus' mother said to him, "They are out of wine." ⁴"You must not tell me what to do, woman," Jesus replied. "My time has not yet come." ⁵Jesus' mother then told the servants, "Do whatever he tells you."

⁶The Jews have religious rules about washing, and for this purpose six stone water jars were there, each one large enough to hold between twenty and thirty gallons. ⁷Jesus said to the servants, "Fill these jars with water." They filled them to the brim, ⁸and then he told them, "Now draw some water out and take it to the man in charge of the feast." They took it to him,

⁹and he tasted the water, which had turned into wine. He did not know where this wine had come from (but the servants who had drawn out the water knew); so he called the bridegroom ¹⁰and said to him, "Everyone else serves the best wine first, and after the guests have drunk a lot he serves the ordinary wine. But you have kept the best wine until now!"

¹¹Jesus performed this first of his mighty works in Cana of Galilee; there he revealed his glory, and his disciples believed in him. ¹²After

this, Jesus and his mother, brothers, and disciples went to Capernaum, and stayed there a
few days.

The miracle at Cana, as a miracle, demonstrates
Jesus' divine power and serves the same purpose as the
witness to his credentials in 1:1–51. It also contains, in
the changing of the water to wine, what has been
called the replacement theme. The miracle symbolizes
the replacement of the old covenant by the new covenant. The waters of purification represent the old covenant and are replaced by the wine which represents
the new covenant. The "best wine," which comes from
Jesus and is served last, points out that Jesus is the one
who brings the new covenant.

The relationship of the new covenant to Jesus' messiahship, which is expressed through the wedding feast
in Cana, can be understood more easily when the
reader realizes that, in the Old Testament, messianic
days of salvation were frequently symbolized by marriage, weddings, and an **abundance** of wine. (This symbolism can be seen in such Old Testament passages as
Hosea 2:14–23 and 14:7, Isaiah 54:4–8 and 62:4–5,
Jeremiah 31:12, Amos 9:13–14, Genesis 49:10–12, where
messianic days and the time of the new covenant are
intimately associated.) As John's Jewish-Christian audience comes to realize that Jesus has miraculously
changed water to wine at the wedding feast, they are
meant to remember these Old Testament passages
and to understand that Jesus is the Messiah and that he
has come from the Father to bring to an end the old
covenant and to inaugurate the new.

There are three important concepts which John uses
not only in this sequence but also throughout the whole
of his Gospel: first, the "sign-miracle" concept which

testifies to the union between Jesus and the Father; second, the "glory-hour" concept which means the glory of the Father will be fully realized in the "hour" of Jesus' passion, death, and resurrection; third, the "belief" concept which expresses credence and trust in Jesus and in the truth of his claims. These three major Johannine concepts are expressed in 2:4,9,11. The observant reader will notice that they recur regularly in the rest of the Gospel.

Sequence 3 (2:13–25)
Jesus' Witness to Himself

Everyone is familiar with the story of the cleansing of the Temple. The incident takes place in Jerusalem at the Jewish Passover. Jesus expels the merchants from the Temple—his Father's house. When the Jews ask Jesus for a miracle to prove his authority, Jesus enters into a dialogue with them about the destruction of the Temple.

Sequence 3 (2:13–25)

[13]It was almost time for the Jewish Feast of Passover, so Jesus went to Jerusalem.

[14]In the Temple he found men selling cattle, sheep, and pigeons, and also the money-changers sitting at their tables. [15]He made a whip from cords and drove all the animals out of the Temple, both the sheep and the cattle; he overturned the tables of the money-changers and scattered their coins; [16]and he ordered the men who sold the pigeons, "Take them out of here! Do not make my Father's house a market place!" [17]His disciples remembered that the scripture says, "My devotion for your house, O God, burns in me like a fire."

[18]The Jews came back at him with a question, "What miracle can you perform to show us that you have the right to do this?" [19]Jesus answered, "Tear down this house of God and in three days I will build it again." [20]"You are going to build it again in three days?" they asked him. "It has taken forty-six years to build this Temple!" [21]But the temple Jesus spoke of was his body.

[22]When he was raised from death, therefore, his disciples remembered that he said this; and they believed the scripture and the words that Jesus had said.

[23]While Jesus was in Jerusalem during the Passover Feast, many believed in him as they saw the mighty works he did. [24]But Jesus did not trust himself to them, because he knew all men well. [25]There was no need for anyone to tell him about men, for he well knew what goes on in their hearts.

The crux of the story is when Jesus declares: "Tear down this Temple, and in three days I will build it again" (2:19). Here John uses his technique of double-meaning words. Three of the words can be understood in two ways: first, the way the Jews understand them; and second, the way Jesus understands them. Notice how differently the following words are understood by the Jews and by Jesus. By "tear down" Jesus means his death; by "this Temple" he means his body; by "build it again" he means his resurrection. For the Jews all three words are understood to refer to the Temple of Jerusalem.

John uses these double-meaning words to lead the way for his misunderstanding technique in 2:20. This technique allows him, very early in the Gospel, to direct his reader's attention to Jesus' death and resurrection. It also allows him to tell his readers that even the apostles did not fully understand Jesus nor fully believe in him until after the resurrection (2:22).

Notice also in this story the usual Johannine themes: **witness to Jesus** (this time Jesus witnesses to himself); **response** (negative); **replacement** (Jesus' body replaces the Temple of Jerusalem as the place of worship for all future believers).

In speaking about the Jewish Passover, the Jewish Temple, and Jesus' claim to rebuild the destroyed Temple, John repeats the **theme of replacement** already introduced in sequence 2 where the wine of the new covenant replaced the water of the old covenant. Here in sequence 3, John tells his audience that Jesus replaces the Temple of Jerusalem and becomes himself the Temple of the new covenant.

John's **theme of response** in 2:23–25 can be compared to the parable of the sower in Mark 4:3–20. In John 2:23–25, the response is like that of those "who hear the message, but the worries about this life, the love for riches, and all other kinds of desires crowd in and choke the message, and they don't bear fruit" (Mark 4:19). This statement will continue to be true of many people in John's Gospel.

The Temple story also allows Jesus to **witness** to himself by testifying to his power over death, a power he will speak about again (5:25–30), and prove indisputably by raising Lazarus from the dead (11:1–44) and by rising himself (20:1–18).

■ Reflection

Think about what "giving witness to Jesus" means in your everyday life. How do you give witness to him by action as well as by word?

Sequence 4 (3:1–21)
Jesus' Discourse to Nicodemus

In sequence 4 (3:1–21), we meet Nicodemus, the typical man on the fence for whom John is writing. The Gospel tells us he was a Jewish leader who belonged to the party of the Pharisees (3:1). Later on in the Gospel Nicodemus defends Jesus against the accusations of the chief priests and the Pharisees (7:45–52). We hear of him for the last time when he assists Joseph of Arimathea in burying Jesus (19:39–42).

The one thing we never find out is whether or not Nicodemus made a decision for Christ and gave up the synagogue. Despite what Nicodemus actually decided in real life, in the Gospel he remains "on the fence" and represents for John the type of person who cannot make a definitive decision for Christ. John is probably talking about people like Nicodemus when he says: "Even then, many Jewish authorities believed in Jesus; but because of the Pharisees they did not talk about it openly, so as not to be expelled from the synagogue. They loved the approval of men rather than the approval of God" (12:42–43).

Sequence 4 (3:1–21)

3 There was a man named Nicodemus, a leader of the Jews, who belonged to the party of the Pharisees. [2]One night he came to Jesus and said to him: "We know, Rabbi, that you are a teacher sent by God. No one could do the mighty works you are doing unless God were with him."

[3]Jesus answered, "I tell you the truth: no one can see the Kingdom of God unless he is born again." [4]"How can a grown man be born again?" Nicodemus asked. "He certainly can-

not enter his mother's womb and be born a second time!" [5]"I tell you the truth," replied Jesus, "that no one can enter the Kingdom of God unless he is born of water and the Spirit. [6]Flesh gives birth to flesh, and Spirit gives birth to spirit. [7]Do not be surprised because I tell you, 'You must all be born again.' [8]The wind blows wherever it wishes; you hear the sound it makes, but you do not know where it comes from or where it is going. It is the same way with everyone who is born of the Spirit." [9]"How can this be?" asked Nicodemus.

[10]Jesus answered: "You are a great teacher of Israel, and you don't know this? [11]I tell you the truth: we speak of what we know, and tell what we have seen—yet none of you is willing to accept our message. [12]You do not believe me when I tell you about the things of this world; how will you ever believe me, then, when I tell you about the things of heaven?

[13]"And no one has ever gone up to heaven except the Son of Man, who came down from heaven. [14]As Moses lifted up the bronze snake on a pole in the desert, in the same way the Son of Man must be lifted up, [15]so that everyone who believes in him may have eternal life. [16]For God loved the world so much that he gave his only Son, so that everyone who believes in him may not die but have eternal life. [17]For God did not send his Son into the world to be its Judge, but to be its Savior. [18]Whoever believes in the Son is not judged; whoever does not believe has already been judged, because he has not believed in God's only Son.

[19]"This is how the judgment works: the light has come into the world, but men love the darkness rather than the light, because they do evil things. [20]And anyone who does evil things

hates the light and will not come to the light, because he does not want his evil deeds to be shown up. ²¹But whoever does what is true comes to the light, in order that the light may show that he did his works in obedience to God."

The sequence begins with Nicodemus declaring his belief that Jesus is "a teacher sent by God," because no one could perform the miracles Jesus performed "unless God were with him" (3:2). As we have seen in 2:23–25, however, belief in Jesus only because of his miracles is not enough. Nicodemus' disclosure of his shallow belief in Jesus enables Jesus to launch into a discourse about what is required for eternal salvation, namely: the acceptance of God's gratuitous gift of faith and eternal life by believing in Jesus and testifying to this belief by being "born again" of water (baptism) and the Spirit (3:5).

It is good to note at this point how John sets up the discourses in his Gospel. The discourses usually begin with a dialogue and then taper off into a monologue. More often than not, a discourse has three main steps. First, it begins with a deeply theological statement which usually contains double-meaning words, allowing the "dialogue" (the person addressed) to understand the word or words in a sense other than that intended by Jesus (as in 3:3). Second, there is an objection to or a misunderstanding of Jesus' words which gives Jesus the opportunity to explain his initial statement more fully (for example, 3:4). Third, Jesus then follows with a monologue explaining the meaning of his profound and mysterious statement (for example, 3:5–21).

In passing, it is advisable to note the critical importance of the discourse to Nicodemus. It is *the* theological discourse of the Gospel. It contains the central message and challenge of the Gospel, namely: either come to Jesus, the light of the world, or remain in the darkness. The reader who studies the discourse carefully and understands its subject matter will have gone a long way toward understanding the Gospel of John as a whole.

Jesus begins his dialogue with an answer to a question which appears to have been posed by Nicodemus: "What must I do to gain eternal life?" His answer, that it is necessary to be born again "of water and the Spirit," contains the key to the mystery of salvation. A person cannot attain the kingdom of God through his or her own efforts. The one who accepts baptism testifies to his or her commitment to Jesus and the Church and to receiving God's free gift of faith, the source of salvation.

Jesus explains in 3:9–21, that this free gift of faith comes through him and through his death on the cross, and that those who accept this gift and believe in him will also receive the gift of eternal life.

In 3:14–17, Jesus speaks about being lifted up as "Moses lifted up the bronze snake on a pole in the desert." In the Old Testament, passages from the book of Numbers 21:4–9 and the book of Wisdom 16:5–7 give a good understanding of the bronze snake of 3:14–17. John's audience was familiar with these texts from Numbers and Wisdom, and their understanding of the texts would enhance considerably the meaning of John's portrait of Nicodemus as someone who believes only because he saw miracles (3:2), of faith and salvation as a free gift from God that has nothing to do with human efforts (3:5–8, 16–17), and of Jesus' insistence that salvation comes through him and that belief in him is necessary for salvation.

Verses 19–21 show that one who believes in Jesus is quite unlike Nicodemus. Nicodemus comes to Jesus in the dark of the night (3:2) but does not believe (3:11). Jesus declares that those who believe love the light and come to him as the light of the world (3:21). Also, Nicodemus sees Jesus as just another teacher among many (3:2). A true believer sees Jesus as the unique and only Son of God (3:18). Verses 16–21 contain an urgent invitation to John's audience to choose freely to come to the light and be saved.

Through the theme of "work" in sequence 4 (3:1–21), John develops for his audience his images of Jesus and the Father. The images John draws for his audience are those of a Father and a Son who love the world with an amazing and everlasting love. The reader who comes away from John's Gospel with these images comes away with a Johannine treasure!

Let us now add another dimension to the understanding of this deeply theological discourse by looking at words and themes of sequence 2 (2:1–12) which recur in sequence 4 (3:1–21). First, **the theme of witness.** In 2:7–9, Jesus witnessed to his divine power by changing water to wine at Cana. In 3:10–13, he witnesses to himself again by stating "we speak of what we know" (3:11). He "knows" because he is the one "who came down from heaven" (3:13). In 2:9, the servant did not know from where the wine had come (it had come from Jesus and the Father—from heaven). In 3:8, no one knows from where the wind comes. Verses 10–13 explain that it comes from heaven through baptism and belief in Jesus.

Second, **the theme of response.** In 2:11, the apostles believe in Jesus. They recognize Jesus' miracle as testimony to the union between Jesus and the Father and as revelatory of Jesus' glory. In 3:1, 20–21, Nicodemus' superficial belief, based only on what he sees Jesus do and not on who Jesus is, makes one realize that whoever "comes to the light" (3:21) responds to Jesus as the disciples did rather than as Nicodemus did.

Third, **the theme of replacement.** In 2:6–10, the water changed to wine symbolizes the replacement of the old covenant by the new covenant. In 3:5, John's Jewish audience is meant to see that as the new wine replaced the old waters of purification, so the waters of baptism symbolizing belief in Jesus replace commitment to the old covenant.

In short, if one reads sequence 2 (2:1–12), while focusing on the themes of witness, response, and replacement, and then reads sequence 4 (3:1–21), one notes first how, by repeating the witness theme, John reminds his readers of the truth that Jesus comes from heaven and is sent by the Father. Second, by contrasting the responses of the disciples and Nicodemus, he impresses upon his audience the need to accept the truth of Jesus' claims. Third, by repeating the replacement theme, he urges upon his readers the necessity of severing their ties with the "old Jewish way" and giving themselves over wholeheartedly to the new covenant, the new baptism, the new Moses, and the new Israel—that is, to Christ and his Church.

■ Reflection
Take a few moments to reflect on what it means being "born spiritually" as distinguished from being "born physically" (John 3:6).

Sequence 5 (3:22—4:3)
The Baptist Reiterates His Witness to Jesus

Sequence 5 (3:22—4:3) begins with some of the Baptist's disciples upset because of Jesus' popularity. They complain to John: "Teacher, you remember the man who was with you on the east side of the Jordan (see 1:28), the one you spoke about? Well, he is baptizing now, and everyone is going to him!" (3:26). The complaints of the Baptist's disciples provide the Baptist with an opportunity to repeat once more what he had already said about Jesus in 1:19–34.

Sequence 5 (3:22—4:3)

²²After this, Jesus and his disciples went to the province of Judea. He spent some time with them there, and baptized. ²³John also was baptizing in Aenon, not far from Salim, because there was plenty of water there. People were going to him and he was baptizing them. (²⁴John had not yet been put in prison.) ²⁵Some of John's disciples began arguing with a Jew about the matter of religious washing. ²⁶So they went to John and told him: "Teacher, you remember the man who was with you on the other side of the Jordan, the one you spoke about? Well, he is baptizing now, and everyone is going to him!"

²⁷John answered: "No one can have anything unless God gives it to him. ²⁸You yourselves are my witnesses that I said, 'I am not the Messiah, but I have been sent ahead of him.'

²⁹"The bridegroom is the one to whom the bride belongs; the bridegroom's friend stands

by and listens, and he is glad when he hears the bridegroom's voice. This is how my own happiness is made complete. [30]He must become more important, while I become less important.

[31]"He who comes from above is greater than all; he who is from the earth belongs to the earth and speaks about earthly matters. He who comes from heaven is above all. [32]He tells what he has seen and heard, but no one accepts his message. [33]Whoever accepts his message proves by this that God is true. [34]The one whom God has sent speaks God's words; for God gives him the fullness of his Spirit. [35]The Father loves his Son and has put everything in his power. [36]Whoever believes in the Son has eternal life; whoever disobeys the Son will never have life, but God's wrath will remain on him forever."

4 The Pharisees heard that Jesus was winning and baptizing more disciples than John. ([2]Actually, Jesus himself did not baptize anyone; only his disciples did.) [3]When Jesus heard what was being said, he left Judea and went back to Galilee;

In sequence 1 (1:19–51), the Baptist declared that he was not the Messiah (1:20). His function, he stated, was to prepare the way for "the Lamb of God, who takes away the sin of the world" (1:29), the one who existed before him (1:30), the one he did not know (1:31,33) until God told him that Jesus was the one "upon whom the Holy Spirit came down" (1:33), the one who stands among them (the Jews) but whom **they do not know** (1:26). This man, the Baptist testified, who baptizes with the Holy Spirit, is the Son of God (1:33–34).

In sequence 5, the Baptist again solemnly reminds his disciples that he (John) is not the Messiah (3:28). He then goes on to testify once more to Jesus by comparing Jesus to a bridegroom and himself to the friend or, as we would say, "the best man" of the bridegroom. This analogy would remind the evangelist's audience of several Old Testament passages which beautifully describe the bride as Israel and the bridegroom as God (for example: Hosea 2:19–23; Jeremiah 2:1–3; 3:19–22; and Isaiah 62:1–7). Against the background of this Old Testament analogy, John's audience was meant to see Jesus as the prophesied messianic bridegroom and themselves as the predicted new covenant Israel of God.

Following his comparison of himself to "the bridegroom's friend," the Baptist makes the solemn declaration: "He must become more important while I become less important" (3:30). He then goes on to explain **why** Jesus must become more important while he becomes less important and why everyone is going to Jesus (3:26).

The reason is that Jesus "comes from above," (that is, from heaven) and, therefore, he is "greater than all" and "above all" (3:31). Jesus "speaks God's words, because God gives him the fullness of his Spirit" (3:34). For these reasons Jesus' testimony is true and must be accepted. Jesus has "everything in his power" (3:35), even the power to give eternal life to those who believe in him (3:36). These truths also give the reason for the Baptist's earlier testimony: "I tell you that he is the Son of God" (1:34). Thus the evangelist repeats and reinforces in sequence 5 (3:22—4:3) the witness the Baptist had given to Jesus in sequence 1 (1:19–51).

Taking into account the fact that the evangelist's audience knew and venerated the Baptist as a true prophet, it is certainly fitting for John to begin and end

Part One of his Gospel with the Baptist's witness to Jesus as the one infinitely greater than himself (1:30) and thus the one to whom they must respond.

A point to notice here is that the first time Jesus starts out for Galilee (1:43—2:12), he travels with no opposition from Jewish leaders. In 4:1–3, however, we get the distinct impression that the Pharisees are out to put obstacles in the way of Jesus' mission. This impression derives from a buildup of which the reader may not have been conscious. It begins in 1:19, when the Jewish authorities (Pharisees) send representatives to John the Baptist. The Baptist tells them they "do not know" Jesus (1:26). This incident is followed by a hostile confrontation in the Temple between Jesus and the Jewish authorities in 2:13–25. Then Nicodemus, a member of the Pharisees' party, cannot bring himself to believe in Jesus (3:1–21). Finally, the reference to those who "disobey the Son" (3:36) is followed immediately by the evangelist's remark in 4:1–3 that when Jesus heard what the Pharisees were saying, he left Judea and went back to Galilee. Jesus' leaving Galilee because of the animosity of the Pharisees prepares the reader for the Pharisees' opposition to Jesus in the rest of the Gospel. This gradual buildup of opposition and hatred on the part of the Pharisees is one example of how masterfully John uses stories to convey his message and at the same time arouse the emotions of his readers.

■ Discussion

1. How does the rite of Baptism help us to see this sacrament as new birth through water and the Spirit?

2. Discuss insights you have gained from the Gospel of John into the great Christian truths of Trinity, incarnation, and redemption.

3. From your personal experience, cite and share instances of situations in which you have had to choose between the way of Christ and the "ways of the world."

4. Reread John 3:16–17. Discuss how this passage may be said to sum up all of salvation history.

5. How is the bronze snake lifted up by Moses an Old Testament a symbol of salvation? Read Numbers 21:4–9; Wisdom 16:5–7; John 3:16–17.

■ Prayer and Meditation

"When terrible, fierce snakes attacked your people and were killing them with their poison, you did not remain angry long enough to destroy your people. This trouble lasted for only a little while, as a warning. Then you gave them a healing symbol, the bronze snake, to remind them of what your Law requires. If a person looked at that symbol, he was cured of the snakebite—not by what he saw, but by you, the savior of mankind."   Wisdom 16:5–7

"As Moses lifted up the bronze snake on a pole in the desert, in the same way the Son of Man must be lifted up, so that everyone who believes in him may have eternal life. For God who loved the world so much that he gave his only Son, so that everyone who believes in him may not die but have eternal life."

John 3:14–16

Part Two
Response to Jesus: Belief and Unbelief
_____ John 4:4—6:15

In our study of the remainder of John's Gospel, we concentrate less on the study of the evangelist's literary techniques and more on the study of his theological message and its meaning for John's audience and the Church in the world of today. We presuppose, however, that the reader will continue to pay attention to the literary techniques. They are vitally important for a correct understanding of John's message.

Relationships

Currently there is much discussion about meaningful relationships. Almost every day we experience different types of relationships and different responses to these relationships. We have, for example, relationships with and responses to family and friends, acquaintances and store clerks, teachers and priests, and so on.

We all know that generous, positive responses not only enable a particular relationship to live but also even to grow into a deeper relationship. An acquaintance becomes a friend, for example, a friend becomes a best friend, a best friend becomes a marriage partner, and so on. Negative responses, on the other hand, may not only curtail the beginnings of a relationship but may also even cause a living relationship to stagnate and perhaps die.

In Part Two of his Gospel (4:4—6:15), John dramatizes magnificently the way Jesus interacts with various people and tries to develop with them relationships based on faith in him. Some accept Jesus by responding positively and believing; others reject him by responding negatively and refusing to believe. The outline of Part Two (sequences 6—10) shows how this drama unfolds. Refer to the chart on page 16:

6—The Samaritan woman believes in Jesus (4:4—38).
7—The Samaritan townspeople believe in Jesus (4:39—45).
8—The government official believes Jesus' promise that his son will live (4:46—54).
9—The Jerusalem Jews refuse to believe in Jesus even though he cures a paralytic (5:1—47).
10—The Galilean Jews, rather than believing in Jesus after the multiplication of the loaves, try instead to take him by force and make him a power-politics Messiah (6:1—15).

■ *Reflection*
Think for a moment how some of your own present relationships have been affected by your responses, positive or negative.

Sequence 6 (4:4—38)
Jesus and the Samaritan Woman

In this sequence, Jesus' aim is to establish a relationship with the Samaritan woman in order to bring her to believe in him and so receive eternal life.

Sequence 6 (4:4—38)

⁴on his way there he had to go through Samaria. ⁵He came to a town in Samaria named Sychar, which was not far from the field that

Jacob had given to his son Joseph. ⁶Jacob's well was there, and Jesus, tired out by the trip, sat down by the well. It was about noon.

⁷A Samaritan woman came to draw some water, and Jesus said to her, "Give me a drink of water." (⁸His disciples had gone into town to buy food.) ⁹The Samaritan woman answered, "You are a Jew and I am a Samaritan—how can you ask me for a drink?" (For Jews will not use the same dishes that Samaritans use.) ¹⁰Jesus answered, "If you only knew what God gives, and who it is that is asking you for a drink, you would have asked him and he would have given you living water." ¹¹"Sir," the woman said, "you don't have a bucket and the well is deep. Where would you get living water? ¹²Our ancestor Jacob gave us this well; he, his sons, and his flocks all drank from it. You don't claim to be greater than Jacob, do you?" ¹³Jesus answered: "Whoever drinks this water will get thirsty again; ¹⁴but whoever drinks the water that I will give him will never be thirsty again. For the water that I will give him will become in him a spring which will provide him with living water, and give him eternal life." ¹⁵"Sir," the woman said, "give me this water! Then I will never be thirsty again, nor will I have to come here and draw water." ¹⁶"Go call your husband," Jesus told her, "and come back here." ¹⁷"I don't have a husband," the woman said. Jesus replied: "You are right when you say you don't have a husband. ¹⁸You have been married to five men, and the man you live with now is not really your husband. You have told me the truth."

¹⁹"I see you are a prophet, sir," the woman said. ²⁰"My Samaritan ancestors worshiped God on this mountain, but you Jews say that Jerusalem is the place where we should wor-

ship God." ²¹Jesus said to her: "Believe me, woman, the time will come when men will not worship the Father either on this mountain or in Jerusalem. ²²You Samaritans do not really know whom you worship; we Jews know whom we worship, for salvation comes from the Jews. ²³But the time is coming, and is already here, when the real worshipers will worship the Father in spirit and in truth. These are the worshipers the Father wants to worship him. ²⁴God is Spirit, and those who worship him must worship in spirit and in truth."

²⁵The woman said to him, "I know that the Messiah, called Christ, will come. When he comes he will tell us everything." ²⁶Jesus answered, "I am he, I who am talking with you." ²⁷At that moment Jesus' disciples returned; and they were greatly surprised to find him talking with a woman. But none of them said to her, "What do you want?" or asked him, "Why are you talking with her?" ²⁸Then the woman left her water jar, went back to town, and said to the people there, ²⁹"Come and see the man who told me everything I have ever done. Could he be the Messiah?" ³⁰So they left the town and went to Jesus. ³¹In the meantime the disciples were begging Jesus, "Teacher, have something to eat!" ³²But he answered, "I have food to eat that you know nothing about." ³³So the disciples started asking among themselves, "Could somebody have brought him food?" ³⁴"My food," Jesus said to them, "is to obey the will of him who sent me and finish the work he gave me to do.

³⁵"You have a saying, 'Four more months and then the harvest.' I tell you, take a good look at the fields: the crops are now ripe and ready to be harvested! ³⁶The man who reaps the harvest is being paid and gathers the crops for

eternal life; so that the man who plants and the man who reaps will be glad together. [37]For the saying is true, 'One man plants, another man reaps.' [38]I have sent you to reap a harvest in a field where you did not work; others worked there, and you profit from their work."

Many commentators have observed that John dramatizes this sequence with all the skill of a modern playwright. It could in fact be staged almost as it stands without further directions. In scene one, Jesus arrives on center stage and sits down. (The apostles are in town buying food.) A Samaritan woman arrives and dialogues with Jesus (4:7–26). When the dialogue ends, the woman exits, and the apostles rejoin Jesus on center stage (4:17–18).

As Jesus dialogues with the apostles, the audience's attention is drawn to a separate stage, the town, where the Samaritan woman in scene two is shown testifying to the townspeople about Jesus (4:27–29) and the townspeople are shown setting off across the fields to see Jesus (4:30). Meanwhile, back on center stage in scene three, Jesus continues to dialogue with his apostles (4:31–38). When the dialogue ends (4:38), the townspeople arrive on center stage, and the scene is set for sequence 7 (4:39–45).

For the reader who has mastered the intricacies of Jesus' discourse to Nicodemus, the scene with the Samaritan woman should be relatively simple. After the opening dialogue (4:7–9), Jesus makes a profound theological statement: "If you only knew **what** God gives and **who** it is that is asking you for a drink, you would ask him, and he would give you life-giving water."

In typical Johannine fashion, the woman is made to misunderstand what Jesus means by life-giving water and to think it is special water that will never give out and will consequently save her the trouble of hauling water from the well every day (4:13–15).

In the monologue which follows (4:21–26), it is taken for granted that John's audience, which has already heard the Nicodemus story in 3:1–21, understands that this marvelous water symbolizes the gift of faith that leads to eternal life. In 4:16–26, therefore, the dialogue deals with the question of *who* it is that is asking the woman for water, and offering her "life-giving" water. The answer, of course, is that it is Jesus, Prophet (4:19) and Messiah (4:25–26).

The reason for Jesus' relationship with the Samaritan woman becomes even clearer in his conversation with his apostles about food (4:31). Jesus' continuing monologue is the clue to the whole scene. He says, "I have food to eat that you know nothing about. My food . . . is to obey the will of the one who sent me and to finish the work he gave me to do" (4:32–34). According to 3:16, the work the Father gave Jesus to do is to bring the world to believe in him and thus attain eternal life. In bringing the Samaritan woman to believe in him, Jesus has been doing the work the Father gave him to do! What Jesus does in 4:31–38 is to urge his apostles to continue this work. As we know, John is directing this story to his fence-straddling audience. The Samaritan woman is meant to be an example to them! Like the Samaritan woman who accepted Jesus and shared her belief by telling her townspeople about him, they are expected to accept Jesus and share their belief in him with others because of **who** Jesus is and because of **what** he offers to all people—eternal life.

■ Reflection

Why do you think that Jesus' promise of eternal life would have a tremendous impact on his hearers and on the audience of John's Gospel? Should it—does it—have the same effect on you and me?

Sequence 7 (4:39–45)
The Samaritan Townspeople Believe in Jesus

What is unique about this story is the townspeople's openness to Jesus. They believe on Jesus' word alone! They do not have to see miracles. They are the kind of people Jesus is speaking about later when he says to doubting Thomas: "Do you believe because you see me? How happy are those who believe without seeing me!" (20:20).

Sequence 7 (4:39–45)

³⁹Many of the Samaritans in that town believed in Jesus because the woman had said, "He told me everything I have ever done."

⁴⁰So when the Samaritans came to him they begged him to stay with them; and Jesus stayed there two days.

⁴¹Many more believed because of his message, ⁴²and they told the woman, "We believe now, not because of what you said, but because we ourselves have heard him, and we know that he is really the Savior of the world."

⁴³After spending two days there, Jesus left and went to Galilee. ⁴⁴For Jesus himself had said, "A prophet is not respected in his own country."

⁴⁵When he arrived in Galilee the people there welcomed him, for they themselves had gone to the Passover Feast in Jerusalem and had seen everything that he had done during the feast.

Faith in Jesus for the majority of Christians down through the centuries has depended on their accepting the gift of faith given to them freely by God rather than on their believing because they have seen miracles. It is very significant, therefore, that John begins this little story by emphasizing that "Many of the Samaritans in that town **believed** in Jesus" (4:39) and ends it by noting, "When he arrived in Galilee, the people [Jews] there **welcomed** him because they had gone to the Passover Festival in Jerusalem and had **seen** everything that he had **done** during the festival" (4:45). The Samaritans **believe!** The Jews of Galilee, however, only **welcome** Jesus, and they welcome him only because they have **seen his miracles.** They **welcome** him, but unlike the Samaritans nothing is said about their **believing.** There is a world of difference between welcoming and believing! In sequences 9 and 10, John continues this theme of negative response by showing the Jews of Jerusalem (5:1–47) and the Jews of Galilee (6:1–15) obstinately refusing to believe in Jesus even after he has performed miracles in their presence!

Sequence 8 (4:46–54)
The Royal Official Believes

The government official, like the Samaritans, is almost certainly non-Jewish. And like the Samaritans, he believes on Jesus' word alone (4:50) without seeing a miracle. To people who think that faith depends on miracles, Jesus says, "None of you will ever believe unless you see miracles and wonders" (4:48).

Sequence 8 (4:46–54)

⁴⁶So Jesus went back to Cana of Galilee, where he had turned the water into wine. There was a government official there whose son in Capernaum was sick.

⁴⁷When he heard that Jesus had come from Judea to Galilee, he went to him and asked him to go to Capernaum and heal his son, who was about to die. ⁴⁸Jesus said to him, "None of you will ever believe unless you see great and wonderful works." ⁴⁹"Sir," replied the official, "come with me before my child dies." ⁵⁰Jesus said to him, "Go, your son will live!"

The man believed Jesus' words and went.

⁵¹On his way home his servants met him with the news, "Your boy is going to live!" ⁵²He asked them what time it was when his son got better, and they said, "It was one o'clock yesterday afternoon when the fever left him." ⁵³The father remembered, then, that it was at that very hour when Jesus had told him, "Your son will live." So he and all his family believed.

⁵⁴This was the second mighty work that Jesus did after coming from Judea to Galilee.

This same story of a Roman officer's belief in Jesus is found in Matthew 8:5–13 and Luke 7:1–10 but with differences. The differences are due to the fact that the original story was passed on by all kinds of preachers and teachers from the time of Christ down to the time when it was picked up and included in the written Gospels. Each evangelist uses the story according to his own theological purposes: Matthew, to emphasize the power and authority of Jesus; Luke, to emphasize the deep faith of the government official. In John's Gospel, the story is told to emphasize for his audience the critical truth that genuine faith in Jesus is based, not on miracles, but on believing in Jesus' word alone. As John will demonstrate in his next two sequences, the cure of the paralytic (5:1–47) and the multiplication of the loaves (6:1–15), even miracles will not bring to belief in Jesus those who love the darkness and refuse to accept the gift of faith offered by God to all.

The official's belief in Jesus, however, is a good example of sincere openness to Jesus. The words, "The man believed Jesus' words" (4:50), coupled with "So he and all his family believed" (4:53), indicate that the official believed in Jesus even before he knew about the miracle. The miracle only confirmed his belief.

In sequence 4 (3:1–21), Jesus offers believers a new life. In sequences 6, 7, and 8, we have seen, respectively, the Samaritan woman, the Samaritan townspeople, and the government official accepting this new life. Their responses are all meant to be examples for John's audience.

■ Reflection

How vital a factor is openness in our personal relationships? How do you show openness to Jesus and others? To Jesus in others?

Sequence 9 (5:1–47)
Jesusalem Refuses to Believe

The scene now shifts to Jerusalem, and the tone of the Gospel changes perceptibly. The reader begins to feel the pathos behind John's statement in the prologue about the relationship between Jesus and his own people: "He came to his own country, but his own people did not receive him" (1:11). The scene takes place at a major festival of the Jews. It opens with Jesus' healing a man who had been sick for a long, long time.

Sequence 9 (5:1–47)

Section One (5:1–18)
Jesus Heals a Paralytic on the Sabbath

5 After this, there was a Jewish religious feast, and Jesus went to Jerusalem. ²There is in Jerusalem, by the Sheep Gate, a pool with five porches; in the Hebrew language it is called Bethzatha. ³A large crowd of sick people were lying on the porches—the blind, the lame, and the paralyzed. [They were waiting for the water to move; ⁴for every now and then an angel of the Lord went down into the pool and stirred up the water. The first sick person to go down into the pool after the water was stirred up was healed from whatever disease he had.] ⁵A man was there who had been sick for thirty-eight years. ⁶Jesus saw him lying there, and he knew that the man had been sick for such a long time; so he said to him, "Do you want to get well?" ⁷The sick man answered, "Sir, I don't have anyone here to put me in the pool when the water is stirred up; while I am trying to get in, somebody else gets there first." ⁸Jesus said to him, "Get up, pick up your mat, and walk." ⁹Immediately the man got well; he picked up his mat, and walked. The day this happened was a Sabbath, ¹⁰so the Jews told the man who had been healed, "This is a Sabbath, and it is against our Law for you to carry your

mat." ¹¹He answered, "The man who made me well told me, 'Pick up your mat and walk.' "

¹²They asked him, "Who is this man who told you to pick up your mat and walk?" ¹³But the man who had been healed did not know who he was, for Jesus had left, because there was a crowd in that place.

¹⁴Afterward, Jesus found him in the Temple and said, "Look, you are well now. Quit your sins, or something worse may happen to you."

¹⁵Then the man left and told the Jews that it was Jesus who had healed him.

¹⁶For this reason the Jews began to persecute Jesus, because he had done this healing on a Sabbath. ¹⁷So Jesus answered them, "My Father works always, and I too must work." ¹⁸This saying made the Jews all the more determined to kill him; for not only had he broken the Sabbath law, but he had said that God was his own Father, and in this way had made himself equal with God.

There is also a story about the cure of a paralytic in Mark 2:1–12, but, as many have observed, John's story is different. In John, the cure takes place in Jerusalem, instead of in Galilee as in Mark, and the precise place is indicated in John: "near the Sheep Gate" where "there is a pool with five porches." Interestingly enough, this pool with the five porches has been excavated in recent years and is now a popular tourist attraction in Jerusalem.

What is more interesting is the way John uses the cure of the paralytic to make his point about faith. He tells the story in nine verses (5:1–9). He then shifts his audience's attention from the miracle to the negative response of the Jewish authorities. They ignore the miracle and blindly object that in curing the paralytic, Jesus has broken the Sabbath work law (5:10–16). Jesus' reply, "My Father is always working, and I too must work" (5:17) enrages them because implicit in these words is his claim that he is equal to the Father. The claim is implicit because Jewish theologians admitted that God alone could work on the Sabbath. Since Jesus claimed that he, too, could work on the Sabbath, the Jewish authorities drew the correct conclusion and accused him of making "himself equal with God" (5:18).

Here, for the first time in John's Gospel, the reader becomes aware not only of the synagogue's opposition to Jesus but also of the underlying reason for the opposition: they refuse to accept Jesus' claim to divinity and instead charge him with blasphemy for claiming to be equal to God! Unlike the positive response of the Samaritan woman, the Samaritan townspeople, and the government official, the response of the Jewish authorities is vehemently negative. Jesus replies to this negative response in a long, accusing monologue in two parts (Sections Two 5:19–30 and Three 5:31–47 which follow).

Section Two (5:19–30)
Jesus' Right to Judge

¹⁹So Jesus answered them: "I tell you the truth: the Son does nothing on his own; he does only what he sees his Father doing. What the Father does, the Son also does. ²⁰For the Father loves the Son and shows him all that he himself is doing. He will show him even greater things than this to do, and you will all be amazed. ²¹For even as the Father raises the dead back to life, in the same way the Son gives life to those he wants to. ²²Nor does the

Father himself judge anyone. He has given his Son the full right to judge, 23so that all will honor the Son in the same way as they honor the Father. Whoever does not honor the Son does not honor the Father who sent him.

24"I tell you the truth: whoever hears my words, and believes in him who sent me, has eternal life. He will not be judged, but has already passed from death to life. 25I tell you the truth: the time is coming—the time has already come—when the dead will hear the voice of the Son of God, and those who hear it will live.

26"Even as the Father is himself the source of life, in the same way he has made his son to be the source of life. 27And he has given the Son the right to judge, because he is the Son of Man.

28"Do not be surprised at this; for the time is coming when all the dead in the graves will hear his voice, 29and they will come out of their graves: those who have done good will be raised and live, and those who have done evil will be raised and be condemned.

30"I can do nothing on my own; I judge only as God tells me, so my judgment is right, because I am not trying to do what I want, but only what he who sent me wants."

Because the Jews ignore the cure of the paralytic, Jesus first reminds them that such a cure shows he has the God-like power to judge. Like a judge, he has the power to give or to take away life (5:19–23). He then solemnly declares that his power to give life is not restricted to the living but at the end of time will be directed even to the dead in their tombs (5:24–30).

For the reader who recalls that John is writing his Gospel for Jews on the fence and is replying to the propaganda of the synagogue against Jesus, the second part of the monologue (5:31–47) is readily understood as a condemnation of those synagogue leaders who have blindly refused to accept Jesus' more than impressive credentials.

Section Three (5:31–47)
Jesus Condemns the Jews of Jerusalem

[31]"If I testify on my own behalf, what I say is not to be accepted as real proof. [32]But there is someone else who testifies on my behalf, and I know that what he says about me is true.

[33]"You sent your messengers to John, and he spoke on behalf of the truth. [34]It is not that I must have a man's witness; I say this only in order that you may be saved. [35]John was like a lamp, burning and shining, and you were willing for a while to enjoy his light.

[36]"But I have a witness on my behalf even greater than the witness that John gave: the works that I do, the works my Father gave me to do, these speak on my behalf and show that the Father has sent me. [37]And the Father, who sent me, also speaks on my behalf. You have never heard his voice, you have never seen his face; [38]so you do not have his words in you, because you will not believe in the one whom he sent. [39]You study the Scriptures because you think that in them you will find eternal life. And they themselves speak about me! [40]Yet you are not willing to come to me in order to have life.

⁴¹"I am not looking for praise from men. ⁴²But I know you; I know that you have no love for God in your hearts. ⁴³I have come with my Father's authority, but you have not received me; when someone comes with his own authority, you will receive him. ⁴⁴You like to have praise from one another, but you do not try to win praise from the only God; how, then, can you believe?

⁴⁵"Do not think, however, that I will accuse you to my Father. Moses is the one who will accuse you—Moses, in whom you have hoped. ⁴⁶If you had really believed Moses, you would have believed me, for he wrote about me. ⁴⁷But since you do not believe what he wrote, how can you believe my words?"

From this point on in the Gospel, John will use all the stories he can about opposition between Jesus and the Jews in order to emphasize the unbelief of the synagogue. Since John himself is a Jew, it should be apparent that his opposition is not to the Jewish people as people but to those among them who were persecuting other Jews who wanted to become Christians. In short, John is not anti-Semitic. He is against anyone who opposes the Word of God and the credentials of Jesus.

John's descriptions of the positive responses of the Samaritans and the government officials are meant as incentives for all people to work towards a deeper relationship with Jesus. They are also meant as warnings against letting faith degenerate into the legalistic and meaningless religion of the Jewish officials.

Sequence 10 (6:1—15)
Negative Response in Galilee

John concludes Part Two of his Gospel with the story of the multiplication of the loaves. It is substantially the same as the story told by Mark (6:35–44), Matthew (14:13–21), and Luke (9:10–17). Unlike the Synoptics, however, John emphasizes not the miracle but the Galilean Jews' rejection of the miracle. Instead of believing in Jesus, the Jews of Galilee hail him as a prophet and try to take him by force to make him a nationalistic king. Jesus, who will later declare before Pilate, "My kingdom does not belong to this world" (18:36), understandably rejects such a response and goes off again to the hills by himself.

Sequence 10 (6:1—15)

6 After this, Jesus went back across Lake Galilee (or, Lake Tiberias, as it is also called). ²A great crowd followed him, because they had seen his mighty works in healing the sick. ³Jesus went up a hill and sat down with his disciples. ⁴The Passover Feast of the Jews was near.

⁵Jesus looked around and saw that a large crowd was coming to him, so he said to Philip, "Where can we buy enough food to feed all these people?" (⁶He said this to try Philip out; actually he already knew what he would do.) ⁷Philip answered, "For all these people to have even a little, it would take more than two hundred dollars' worth of bread." ⁸Another one of his disciples, Andrew, Simon Peter's brother, said: ⁹"There is a boy here who has five loaves of barley bread and two fish. But what good are they for all these people?" ¹⁰"Make the people sit down," Jesus told them.

(There was a lot of grass there.)

So all the people sat down; there were about five thousand men. [11]Jesus took the bread, gave thanks to God, and distributed it to the people sitting down. He did the same with the fish, and they all had as much as they wanted. [12]When they were all full, he said to his disciples, "Pick up the pieces left over; let us not waste a bit." [13]So they took them all up, and filled twelve baskets with the pieces left over from the five barley loaves which the people had eaten.

[14]The people there, seeing this mighty work that Jesus had done, said, "Surely this is the Prophet who was to come into the world!" [15]Jesus knew that they were about to come and get him and make him king by force; so he went off again to the hills by himself.

Relationships cannot be established unless a sense of openness exists between individuals. John shows in the story of the multiplication of the loaves and fishes that the Galilean Jews were not open to Jesus. He positions the story at this point in his Gospel for three good reasons. First, it fits in with his purpose in Part Two (4:4—6:15) of his Gospel, which is to emphasize the theme of response. He has already contrasted the positive responses of such non-Jews as the Samaritan woman, the Samaritan townspeople, and the government official with the negative response of the Jews in Jerusalem. Now, in his version of the loaves miracle, he continues the contrast by showing the negative response of the Jews in Galilee. Second, in Part Four (6:22—12:11) of John's Gospel, Jesus is to give a long discourse on the Eucharist, and John wants his audience to see the loaves miracle as the symbolic counterpart to the Eucharist. The loaves, therefore, serve as an excellent foreshadowing of the bread from heaven in the eucharistic discourse. As Jesus will point out in sequence 12 (6:22—71), the manna in the desert in the time of Moses was not the real bread of life. Only the flesh and blood of Jesus in the Eucharist is the **real** bread of life because the Eucharist gives **eternal** life! Third, as we will now see, the loaves miracle sets the scene for sequence 11 (6:16—21), because of its association with the walking-on-the-sea miracle which John uses as the turning point of his Gospel.

Part Three
Sequence 11 (6:16—21)
Jesus Walks on the Sea

As shown in the chart on page 16, Part Three of John's Gospel has only one sequence. The sequence (number 11) marks the turning point of the Gospel.

11—Jesus walks on the sea (6:16—21).

So far John has shown his fence-straddling audience how the Samaritans and the gentiles recognized Jesus' credentials and believed in him, while the Jews of Jerusalem and Galilee neither recognized nor believed in him.

Now, in six short verses (6:16—21), John hits the members of his audience at the heart of their Jewishness. He takes them back to Moses and the exodus and shows them that it is through Christ and the Church that the promises made to the patriarchs are being fulfilled.

Sequence 11 (6:16–21)

[16]When evening came, his disciples went down to the lake, [17]got into the boat, and went back across the lake toward Capernaum.

Night came on, and Jesus still had not come to them.

[18]By now a strong wind was blowing and stirring up the water.

[19]The disciples had rowed about three or four miles when they saw Jesus walking on the water, coming near the boat, and they were terrified. [20]"Don't be afraid," Jesus told them, "it is I!"

[21]They were willing to take him into the boat; and immediately the boat reached land at the place they were heading for.

In this sequence Jesus walks on the waters of the lake of Galilee and brings his apostles safely through the storm to the opposite shore. To us the incident may seem to be only one of the many miracles of Jesus. To John and to his Jewish audience, however, it is something a great deal more. It is filled with symbolism and packed with Old Testament meaning. It is, in fact, a redramatization of the most sacred event in Israel's history—the exodus. If you compare John 6:16–21 with Exodus 3:15 and 14:1–31 (as follows), you will notice that the parallels shown in the chart stand out with unexpected clarity.

Exodus	John
• Moses is **afraid** (3:6)	• The disciples are **afraid** (6:19).
• God identifies himself as **"I Am"** (3:14).	• Jesus identifies himself as God when he says, "It is I," which has the same meaning as **"I Am"** (6:20).
• The Exodus miracle takes place **at night** and **on the sea** (14:20).	• Jesus comes to the disciples **at night** and **on the sea** (6:16–17).
• God's presence is made known to the Israelites by a **strong wind** (14:21).	• When Jesus comes to the disciples, there is a **strong wind** (6:18).
• God brings the **Israelites** safely to the **other side of the sea** (14:29).	• Jesus brings the disciples (the **new Israel**) to the **other side of the sea** (6:21).
• Because of **God's power over the water,** the Israelites **believe** in the Lord and in Moses (14:31).	• After Jesus (who is God) demonstrates his **power** by walking on **the water,** the disciples willingly take him into the boat—a symbol of their **belief** in him (6:21).

The Johannine theme of replacement becomes clear when one realizes that this episode is a dramatization of an "exodus"—a new exodus which constitutes as the true Israel those who believe in Jesus. Responsive Israel (the believing disciples) through this symbolic new exodus is shown as replacing unresponsive Israel (the unbelieving Jews) and thus becomes the true Israel of God—the Christian Church.

The new Israel's positive response is symbolized by the words, "They willingly took him into the boat" (6:21a), in response to Jesus' words, "It is I!" [that is, "I am God"]: see Exodus 3:14; Deuteronomy 32:39; Isaiah 41:4, 43:10–25, 48:12).

The words, "Then they willingly took him into the boat," are peculiar to John's account. Mark says, "Then he got into the boat with them" (6:51). Matthew says, "They both [Peter and Jesus] got into the boat" (14:32). John, however, emphasizes the positive response of the new Israel by saying, "they **willingly** took him," thus contrasting the positive response of the true Israel with the negative response of the Jews from Jerusalem and Galilee (5:17–47; 6:14–15). It is only fitting in a new exodus account that the new Israel should show its willingness to accept its Redeemer.

To enhance the exodus aspect of the story, John has flanked it on the one side with the loaves episode (6:1–15), which takes place **in the wilderness, near the time of the Passover,** and **on a mountain,** thus evoking remembrance of the gift of manna from heaven, the forty years in the wilderness, the Passover (exodus), and Mount Sinai itself. On the other side, he has flanked it with the great eucharistic discourse (6:22–71), which similarly takes place near the time of the Passover, explicitly mentions Israel's ancestors, the figure of Moses, and the gift of 'bread' (manna) from heaven. In short, John has evoked memories of the old exodus to emphasize in the turning point of his Gospel that a new exodus has taken place and a new people of God has come into existence.

John's is not the only Gospel that has a turning point. What Jesus does in John 6:16–21 is similar to what he does in the turning points of Matthew, Mark, and Luke: he turns **away from** those who have rejected him and turns **to** those who have accepted him. In Matthew's Gospel, the turning point is in chapters 10–13, where the Jews reject Jesus, who then turns to his apostles and instructs them on the meaning of the true Church. In Mark's Gospel, following Jesus' disputes with the Pharisees after his two multiplications of the loaves and immediately after Peter's acceptance of him as Messiah (8:27–30), Jesus turns away from the unbelieving Pharisees and begins to instruct his disciples on the essentials of discipleship. In Luke's Gospel, the turning point occurs in 9:52, when Jesus "turns" his face toward Jerusalem and death and then, in the course of his journey to Jerusalem, instructs his disciples on what it means to "follow" him.

In Part Four (6:22–12:11) of his Gospel, John shows Jesus again and again turning away from the hostile Jews and refuting their objections to him personally and to the beliefs of the Christian Church. In Part Five (12:12–21:25), and especially in Jesus' long farewell discourse (chapters 13–17), John shows Jesus turning to his disciples and instructing them on the essentials of discipleship.

■ Discussion

1. What are some specific ways in which we can share our belief in Jesus with others?

2. Discuss insights you have gained from this study session into the great truth that Jesus is Son of God and Son of Man.

■ Prayer and Meditation

"As a deer longs for a stream of cool water,
so I long for you, O God.
I thirst for you, the living God."

Psalm 42:1–2

"Whoever drinks this water will get thirsty again but whoever drinks the water that I will give him will never be thirsty again. The water that I will give him will become in him a spring which will provide him with life-giving water and give him eternal life."

John 4:13–14

Part Four Controversy About Jesus' Credentials ___ John 6:22—10:21

In the first two study sessions, we have seen that Part One of John's Gospel centers around the presentation of Jesus' credentials as Son of God and Messiah, and Part Two deals with positive and negative responses to Jesus' credentials. Part Three dramatizes the new exodus, the turning point in John's Gospel.

Part Four (6:22—12:11) deals with the controversy about Jesus' credentials. When we look at it not just as Part Four but also as Act Four in the drama of the Gospel of John, we can describe the overall stage setting as an informal trial acted out in successive scenes (sequences 12–16) as follows:

12—In the great eucharistic discourse, Jesus defends his declaration that he is the bread of life (6:22–71).
13—In Jerusalem at the Festival of Shelters, Jesus defends his teaching authority, messiahship, and divinity (7:1—8:59).
14—Still at the Festival of Shelters, Jesus cures the man born blind, exposes the blindness of the Pharisees, and brands them as "hired" shepherds (9:1—10:21).
15—In Jerusalem at the Festival of the Dedication of the Temple, Jesus once again defends his messiahship and divinity (10:22–39).

16—In Bethany, Jesus raises Lazarus and gives the ultimate proof of his power over life and death (10:40—12:11).

These sequences are linked internally by the continuing controversy between Jesus and the Jews and by the increasingly hostile response of the Jewish leaders: they scorn Jesus in 6:22–71; they want to stone him to death in 7:1—8:58; they ignore his miracle in 9:1—10:21; they try again to stone him in 10:22–39; finally, they plot his death in 10:40—12:11. The picture John presents of the Jewish leaders is not flattering; nor is it meant to be. He wants his readers, especially those on the fence, to see the synagogue and its leaders in their true colors.

Study Session Three here covers sequences 12, 13, and 14 of Part Four of the Gospel of John (refer once more to your chart on page 16). Study Session Four covers sequences 15 and 16.

Sequence 12 (6:22–71)
The Discourse on the Eucharist

In the great eucharistic discourse (6:22–71), we find the Jews of Galilee scorning Jesus' claim that he is the true bread come down from heaven and that whoever eats this bread will live forever. Here, then, as in a courtroom trial, Jesus defends his presence in the Eucharist by arguing that if the Father, through Moses, can send manna from heaven for earthly life, the Father can with equal reason send him (Jesus) from heaven as the bread of eternal life.

Sequence 12 (6:22–71)

²²Next day the crowd which had stayed on the other side of the lake saw that only one boat was left there. They knew that Jesus had

69

not gone in the boat with his disciples, but that they had left without him. ²³Other boats, from Tiberias, came to shore near the place where the crowd had eaten the bread, after the Lord had given thanks. ²⁴When the crowd saw that Jesus was not there, nor his disciples, they got into boats and went to Capernaum, looking for him.

²⁵When the people found Jesus on the other side of the lake they said to him, "Teacher, when did you get here?" ²⁶Jesus answered: "I tell you the truth: you are looking for me because you ate the bread and had all you wanted, not because you saw my works of power. ²⁷Do not work for food that spoils; instead, work for the food that lasts for eternal life. This food the Son of Man will give you, because God, the Father, has put his mark of approval on him." ²⁸They asked him then, "What can we do in order to do God's works?" ²⁹Jesus answered, "This is the work God wants you to do: believe in the one he sent." ³⁰They replied: "What sign of power will you perform so that we may see it and believe you? What will you do? ³¹Our ancestors ate manna in the desert, just as the scripture says: 'He gave them bread from heaven to eat.' " ³²"I tell you the truth," Jesus said. "What Moses gave you was not the bread from heaven; it is my Father who gives you the real bread from heaven. ³³For the bread that God gives is he who comes down from heaven and gives life to the world." ³⁴"Sir," they asked him, "give us this bread always." ³⁵"I am the bread of life," Jesus told them. "He who comes to me will never be hungry; he who believes in me will never be thirsty. ³⁶Now, I told you that you had seen me but would not believe. ³⁷Every one whom my Father gives me will come to me. I will never turn away anyone

who comes to me, [38]for I have come down from heaven to do the will of him who sent me, not my own will. [39]This is what he who sent me wants me to do: that I should not lose any of all those he has given me, but that I should raise them all to life on the last day. [40]For this is what my Father wants: that all who see the Son and believe in him should have eternal life; and I will raise them to life on the last day."

[41]The Jews started grumbling about him, because he said, "I am the bread that came down from heaven." [42]So they said: "This man is Jesus, the son of Joseph, isn't he? We know his father and mother. How, then, does he now say he came down from heaven?"

[43]Jesus answered: "Stop grumbling among yourselves. [44]No one can come to me unless the Father who sent me draws him to me; and I will raise him to life on the last day. [45]The prophets wrote, 'All men will be taught by God.' Everyone who hears the Father and learns from him comes to me. [46]This does not mean that anyone has seen the Father; he who is from God is the only one who has seen the Father. [47]I tell you the truth: he who believes has eternal life. [48]I am the bread of life. [49]Your ancestors ate the manna in the desert, but died. [50]But the bread which comes down from heaven is such that whoever eats it will not die. [51]I am the living bread which came down from heaven. If anyone eats this bread he will live forever. And the bread which I will give him is my flesh, which I give so that the world may live." [52]This started an angry argument among the Jews. "How can this man give us his flesh to eat?" they asked. [53]Jesus said to them: "I tell you the truth: if you do not eat the flesh of the Son of Man and drink his blood you will not

have life in yourselves. [54]Whoever eats my flesh and drinks my blood has eternal life, and I will raise him to life on the last day. [55]For my flesh is the real food, my blood is the real drink. [56]Whoever eats my flesh and drinks my blood lives in me and I live in him. [57]The living Father sent me, and because of him I live also. In the same way, whoever eats me will live because of me. [58]This, then, is the bread that came down from heaven; it is not like the bread that your ancestors ate and then died. The one who eats this bread will live forever."

[59]Jesus said this as he taught in the synagogue in Capernaum. [60]Many of his disciples heard this and said, "This teaching is too hard. Who can listen to this?" [61]Without being told, Jesus knew that his disciples were grumbling about this; so he said to them: "Does this make you want to give up? [62]Suppose, then, that you should see the Son of Man go back up to the place where he was before? [63]What gives life is the Spirit; the flesh is of no use at all. The words I have spoken to you are Spirit and life. [64]Yet some of you do not believe." (For Jesus knew from the very beginning who were the ones that would not believe, and which one would betray him.) [65]And he added, "This is the very reason I told you that no one can come to me unless the Father makes it possible for him to do so." [66]Because of this, many of his followers turned back and would not go with him any more. [67]So Jesus said to the twelve disciples, "And you—would you like to leave also?" [68]Simon Peter answered him: "Lord, to whom would we go? You have the words that give eternal life. [69]And now we believe and know that you are the Holy One from God." [70]Jesus answered them, "Did I not choose the twelve of you? Yet one of you is a devil!" [71]He was talking

about Judas, the son of Simon Iscariot. For Judas, even though he was one of the twelve disciples, was going to betray him.

The crowd's request for a miracle in 6:30 (as though Jesus had not already performed one!) sets the scene for Jesus' great eucharistic discourse. In this discourse (6:31–58), Jesus asks his hearers to believe what he says simply because he says it, that is, he asks them to believe on his word alone. Notice how Jesus disregards their request for a miracle and goes on to use such words as "telling," "told," "taught," and "hears," thus emphasizing the theme of believing on his **word** alone.

What Jesus actually does in the eucharistic discourse (6:31–58) is give a homily on the text cited in 6:31: "He gave them bread from heaven to eat." In Jewish homilies of the time, it was the practice to first cite the text of the homily and then explain each word of the text. In Jesus' homily, the text is given in 6:31. Then Jesus explains each word of the text. In 6:32, he explains the words "he gave" as the Father gave—not Moses. In 6:33, he explains "bread from heaven" as "he who comes down from heaven and gives life to the world," that is, as himself. In 6:35–48, he explains the word "them" as "he who comes to us" (6:35) and as "everyone whom my Father gives me" (6:36–40 and 6:43–47). He explains the important words "to eat" in 6:48–58, first, as his own "flesh" which he gives "so that the world may live" (6:51), and then as "real food" (6:55), "not like the bread [their] ancestors ate but then later died," but rather as the bread which will enable them to "live forever" (6:58).

Consider the sequence of events we have just seen. First, Jesus feeds five thousand with five loaves and two fish (6:1–15). Then he performs a miracle for his disciples by walking on the water (6:16–21). Finally, in sequence 12 (6:22–71), the crowds who ate the bread at the multiplication of the loaves ask Jesus what they must do in order to do what God desires of them (6:28). Jesus answers, "What God wants you to do is to believe in the one he sent." The reaction of the Jews and even of many of Jesus' followers to this request is found in 6:60–71. Many of them found this teaching "too hard" and "would not go with him any more" (6:66). Thus we see that the Church's age-old belief in Jesus' bodily eucharistic presence was a difficult doctrine from the beginning.

It is the responses, therefore, to Jesus' eucharistic defense that John wishes to emphasize for his audience: first, the negative response of many of Jesus' followers who said, "This teaching is too hard. Who can listen to it?"; second, the response of Simon Peter, which is the response that John wishes to elicit from his audience. When Jesus asks, "Would you also like to leave?" Simon Peter, as spokesman for the apostles, replies, "Lord, to whom would we go?" The reasoning behind this response is even more important for John. Peter proclaims that they must follow Jesus because he is "the Holy One who has come from God." John's ever-recurring theme of the necessity of believing in Jesus because of **who** he is and **what** he says is once again stated here. Like the Samaritan woman, the Samaritan townspeople, and the government official, Peter and the apostles believe in Jesus on his word alone.

■ Reflection
Why does the Church in its prayer call the Eucharist "a pledge of the glory to come"?

Do you at times find it difficult to do what God desires of you? Share your experience with others.

Sequence 13 (7:1—8:59)
Jesus' Witness to Himself

Sequence 13 opens with a scene in Galilee showing Jesus' own people still not believing in him (7:1–9). The scene then shifts to Jerusalem, where the crowds at the Festival of Shelters discuss whether or not they should believe in Jesus. The Jewish leaders try first to arrest Jesus and then to stone him.

Sequence 13 (7:1—8:59)

7 After this, Jesus traveled in Galilee; he did not want to travel in Judea, because the Jews there were wanting to kill him. ²The Jewish Feast of Tabernacles was near, ³so Jesus' brothers said to him: "Leave this place and go to Judea, so that your disciples will see the works you are doing. ⁴No one hides what he is doing if he wants to be well known. Since you are doing these things, let the whole world know about you!" (⁵Not even his brothers believed in him.) ⁶Jesus said to them: "The right time for me has not yet come. Any time is right for you. ⁷The world cannot hate you, but it hates me, because I keep telling it that its ways are bad. ⁸You go on to the feast. I am not going to this feast, because the right time has not come for me." ⁹He told them this, and stayed on in Galilee. ¹⁰After his brothers went to the feast, Jesus also went; however, he did not go openly, but went secretly. ¹¹The Jews were looking for him at the feast. "Where is he?" they asked. ¹²There was much whispering about him in the crowd. "He is a good man," some people said. "No," others said, "he fools the people." ¹³But no one talked about him openly, because they were afraid of the Jews. ¹⁴The feast was nearly half over when Jesus went to the Temple and began teaching. [15]The Jews, greatly surprised, said, "How does this man know so much when he has never been to school?" [16]Jesus answered: "What I teach is not mine, but comes from God, who sent me. [17]Whoever is willing to do what God wants will know whether what I teach comes from God or whether I speak on my own authority. [18]A person who speaks on his own is trying to gain glory for himself. He who wants glory for the one who sent him, however, is honest and there is nothing false in him. [19]Moses gave you the Law, did he not? But not one of you obeys the Law. Why are you trying to kill me?" [20]The crowd answered, "You have a demon in you! Who is trying to kill you?" [21]Jesus answered: "I did one great work and you were all surprised. [22]Because Moses ordered you to circumcise your sons (although it was not Moses but your ancestors who started it), you will circumcise a boy on the Sabbath. [23]If a boy is circumcised on the Sabbath so that Moses' Law will not be broken, why are you angry with me because I made a man completely well on the Sabbath? [24]Stop judging by external standards, but judge by true standards." [25]Some of the people of Jerusalem said: "Isn't this the man they are trying to kill? [26]Look! He is talking in public, and nobody says anything against him! Can it be that the leaders really know that he is the Messiah? [27]But when the Messiah comes, no one will know where he is from. And we all know where this man comes from." [28]As Jesus taught in the Temple he said in a loud voice: "Do you really know me, and know where I am from? But I have not come on my own. He who sent me, however, is true. You do not know him, [29]but I know him, for I come from him and he sent me." [30]Then they tried to arrest him, but no one laid a hand on him, because his hour had not yet come. [31]But many in the crowd believed in him, and said, "When the Messiah comes, will he do more mighty works than this man has done?" [32]The Pharisees heard the crowd whispering these things about him, so they and the chief priests sent some guards to arrest Jesus. [33]Jesus said: "I shall be with you a little while longer, and then I shall go away to him who sent me. [34]You will look for me, but you will not find me; for where I shall be you cannot go." [35]The Jews said among themselves: "Where is he about to go so that we shall not find him? Will he go to the Greek cities where the Jews live and teach the Greeks? [36]He says, 'You will look for me but you will not find me,' and, 'You cannot go where I shall be.' What does he mean?"

[37]The last day of the feast was the most important. On that day Jesus stood up and said in a loud voice: "Whoever is thirsty should come to me and drink. [38]As the scripture says, 'Whoever believes in me, streams of living water will pour out from his heart.' " ([39]Jesus said this about the Spirit which those who believed in him were about to receive. At that time the Spirit had not yet been given, because Jesus had not been raised to glory.) [40]Many of the people in the crowd heard him say this and said, "This man is really the Prophet!" [41]Others said, "He is the Messiah!" But others said, "The Messiah will not come from Galilee! [42]The scripture says that the Messiah will be a descendant of David, and will be born in Bethlehem, the town where David lived." [43]So there was a division in the crowd because of him. [44]Some wanted to arrest him, but no one laid a hand on him.

[45]The guards went back to the chief priests and Pharisees, who asked them, "Why did you

not bring him along?" [46]The guards answered, "Nobody has ever talked the way this man does!" [47]"Did he fool you, too?" the Pharisees asked them. [48]"Have you ever known one of our leaders or one Pharisee to believe in him? [49]This crowd does not know the Law of Moses, so they are under God's curse!" [50]Nicodemus was one of them; he was the one who had gone to see Jesus before. He said to them, [51]"According to our Law we cannot condemn a man before hearing him and finding out what he has done." [52]"Well," they answered, "are you also from Galilee? Study the Scriptures and you will learn that no prophet ever comes from Galilee."

Note to Reader: This story (8:1–11) is not found in the earliest Greek manuscripts and is therefore considered by scholars to be a later addition to the Gospel.

The Woman Caught in Adultery

8 [Then everyone went home, but Jesus went to the Mount of Olives. [2]Early the next morning he went back to the Temple. The whole crowd gathered around him, and he sat down and began to teach them. [3]The teachers of the Law and the Pharisees brought in a woman who had been caught committing adultery, and made her stand before them all. [4]"Teacher," they said to Jesus, "this woman was caught in the very act of committing adultery. [5]In our Law Moses gave a commandment that such a woman must be stoned to death. Now, what do you say?" [6]They said this to trap him, so they could accuse him. But Jesus bent over and wrote on the ground with his finger. [7]As they stood there asking questions, Jesus straightened up and said to them, "Whichever one of you has committed no sin may throw the first stone at her." [8]Then he bent over again and wrote on the ground. [9]When they heard this they all left, one by one, the older ones first. Jesus was left alone, with the woman still standing there. [10]He straightened up and said to her, "Where are they, woman? Is there no one left to condemn you?" "No one, sir," she answered. "Well, then," Jesus said, "I do not [11]condemn you either. You may leave, but do not sin again."]

[12]Jesus spoke to them again: "I am the light of the world. Whoever follows me will have the light of life and will never walk in the darkness." [13]The Pharisees said to him, "Now you are testifying on your own behalf; what you say proves nothing." [14]"No," Jesus answered, "even if I do testify on my own behalf, what I say is true, because I know where I came from and where I am going. You do not know where I came from or where I am going. [15]You make judgments in a purely human way; I pass judgment on no one. [16]But if I were to pass judgment, my judging would be true, because I am not alone in this; the Father who sent me is with me. [17]It is written in your Law that when two witnesses agree, what they say is true. [18]I testify on my own behalf, and the Father who sent me also testifies on my behalf." [19]"Where is your father?" they asked him. "You know neither me nor my Father," Jesus answered. "If you knew me you would know my Father also." [20]Jesus said all this as he taught in the Temple, in the room where the offering boxes

were placed. And no one arrested him, because his hour had not come.

²¹Jesus said to them again, "I will go away; you will look for me, but you will die in your sins. You cannot go where I am going." ²²So the Jews said, "He says, 'You cannot go where I am going.' Does this mean that he will kill himself?" ²³Jesus answered: "You come from here below, but I come from above. You come from this world, but I do not come from this world. ²⁴That is why I told you that you will die in your sins. And you will die in your sins if you do not believe that 'I Am Who I Am'." ²⁵"Who are you?" they asked him. Jesus answered: "What I have told you from the very beginning. ²⁶There are many things I have to say and judge about you. The one who sent me, however, is true, and I tell the world only what I have heard from him." ²⁷They did not understand that he was talking to them about the Father. ²⁸So Jesus said to them: "When you lift up the Son of Man you will know that 'I Am Who I Am'; then you will know that I do nothing on my own, but say only what the Father has taught me. ²⁹And he who sent me is with me; he has not left me alone, because I always do what pleases him." ³⁰Many who heard Jesus say these things believed in him. ³¹So Jesus said to the Jews who believed in him, "If you obey my teaching you are really my disciples; ³²you will know the truth, and the truth will make you free." ³³"We are the descendants of Abraham," they answered, "and we have never been anybody's slaves. What do you mean, then, by saying, 'You will be made free'?" ³⁴Jesus said to them: "I tell you the truth: everyone who sins is a slave of sin. ³⁵A slave does not belong to the family always; but a son belongs there forever. ³⁶If the Son makes you free, then you

will be really free. ³⁷I know you are Abraham's descendants. Yet you are trying to kill me, because you will not accept my teaching. ³⁸I talk about what my Father has shown me, but you do what your father has told you." ³⁹They answered him, "Our father is Abraham." "If you really were Abraham's children," Jesus replied, "you would do the same works that he did. ⁴⁰But all I have ever done is to tell you the truth I heard from God. Yet you are trying to kill me. Abraham did nothing like this! ⁴¹You are doing what your father did." "We are not bastards," they answered. "We have the one Father, God himself." ⁴²Jesus said to them: "If God really were your father, you would love me; for I came from God and now I am here. I did not come on my own, but he sent me. ⁴³Why do you not understand what I say? It is because you cannot bear to listen to my message. ⁴⁴You are the children of your father, the Devil, and you want to follow your father's desires. From the very beginning he was a murderer. He has never been on the side of truth, because there is no truth in him. When he tells a lie he is only doing what is natural to him, because he is a liar and the father of all lies. ⁴⁵I tell the truth, and that is why you do not believe me. ⁴⁶Which one of you can prove that I am guilty of sin? If I tell the truth, then why do you not believe me? ⁴⁷He who comes from God listens to God's words. You, however, are not from God, and this is why you will not listen." ⁴⁸The Jews replied to Jesus: "Were we not right in saying that you are a Samaritan and have a demon in you?" ⁴⁹"I have no demon," Jesus answered. "I honor my Father, but you dishonor me. ⁵⁰I am not seeking honor for myself. There is one who is seeking it and who judges in my favor. ⁵¹I tell you the truth: whoever obeys my message will never die." ⁵²The Jews said to him: "Now we know for sure that you have a demon! Abraham died, and the prophets died, yet you say, 'Whoever obeys my message will never die.' [53]Our father Abraham died; you do not claim to be greater than Abraham, do you? And the prophets also died. Who do you think you are?" [54]Jesus answered: "If I were to honor myself, my own honor would be worth nothing. The one who honors me is my Father—the very one you say is your God. [55]You have never known him, but I know him. If I were to say that I do not know him, I would be a liar, like you. But I do know him, and I obey his word. [56]Your father Abraham rejoiced that he was to see my day; he saw it and was glad." [57]The Jews said to him, "You are not even fifty years old—and you have seen Abraham?" [58]"I tell you the truth," Jesus replied. "Before Abraham was born, 'I Am'." [59]They picked up stones to throw at him; but Jesus hid himself and left the Temple.

The trial motif in this sequence commences at 7:14 and deals with the Jewish leaders' denial of Jesus' teaching authority and messiahship. They deny Jesus' authority to teach because he has not attended a rabbinical school (7:14–15). Jesus agrees concerning his schooling but refutes their opposition to his teaching authority by declaring that his authority comes from a higher source. It comes directly from the Father himself.

The Jewish leaders, far from accepting Jesus' claim to a teaching authority given to him from above, make further accusations against him. They accuse him of: not coming from God because he broke the Sabbath (7:16–24); falsely claiming to be the Messiah (7:25–31, 40–42, 52); illegally testifying on his own behalf (8:13); being possessed by the devil (8:48–52); lying not only about being greater than Abraham, but about living before Abraham was born (8:54–58).

In reply, Jesus defends himself against each accusation. He solemnly declares: he comes from the Father **(passim)**; he is the Messiah who comes from heaven (7:25–52); his testimony is valid because the Father also testifies for him (8:12–20); he is not possessed but is doing the work of the Father (8:48–51); he really existed before Abraham because he is God, that is, he is "I Am" (8:52–58).

Jesus' effort, however, is futile. The Jewish leaders refuse to believe. In the end, some want to seize him (7:30–40); others want to arrest him (7:32, 8:20); still others want to stone him (8:59).

So, in this sequence, John exposes the hard-nosed obstinacy of the Jewish leaders. They will not accept Jesus' word, no matter how impressive his credentials. In the story of the blind man and the good shepherd which follow in the next sequence, John shows how such a hard-nosed refusal to believe arises from that same willful moral blindness of the Pharisees which makes them such bad shepherds of the flock of Israel.

Sequence 14 (9:1—10:21) The Blind Man and the Good Shepherd

The cure of the man born blind, which opens sequence 14 (9:1—10:21), begins with a dialogue between Jesus and his disciples concerning the origin of the man's blindness. Contrary to popular opinion that sickness and disease are the results of sin, Jesus declares that the man's blindness has nothing to do with sin but serves as an occasion for the manifestation of God's power. The sequence has two closely interconnected sections: the story of the blind man (9:1–38) and the parable of the good shepherd (9:39—10:31). We deal first with section one (9:1–38).

Sequence 14 (9:1—10:21)

Section One (9:1–38)
The Pharisees' Refusal to Believe

9 As Jesus walked along he saw a man who had been born blind. [2]His disciples asked him: "Teacher, whose sin was it that caused him to be born blind? His own or his parents' sin?" [3]Jesus answered: "His blindness has nothing to do with his sins or his parents' sins. He is blind so that God's power might be seen at work in him. [4]We must keep on doing the works of him who sent me, as long as it is day; the night is coming, when no one can work. [5]While I am in the world I am the light for the world." [6]After he said this, Jesus spat on the ground and made some mud with the spittle; he rubbed the mud on the man's eyes, [7]and told him, "Go wash your face in the Pool of Siloam." (This name means "Sent.") So the man went, washed his face, and came back seeing.

[8]His neighbors, then, and the people who had seen him begging before this, asked, "Isn't this the man who used to sit and beg?" [9]Some said, "He is the one," but others said, "No, he is not, he just looks like him." So the man himself said, "I am the man." [10]"How were your eyes opened?" they asked him. [11]He answered, "The man named Jesus made some mud, rubbed it on my eyes, and told me, 'Go to Siloam and wash your face.' So I went, and as

soon as I washed I could see." 12"Where is he?" they asked. "I do not know," he answered. 13Then they took the man who had been blind to the Pharisees. 14The day that Jesus made the mud and opened the man's eyes was a Sabbath. 15The Pharisees, then, asked the man again how he had received his sight. He told them, "He put some mud on my eyes, I washed my face, and now I can see." 16Some of the Pharisees said, "The man who did this cannot be from God because he does not obey the Sabbath law." Others, however, said, "How could a man who is a sinner do such mighty works as these?" And there was a division among them. 17So the Pharisees asked the man once more, "You say he opened your eyes—well, what do you say about him?" "He is a prophet," he answered.

18The Jews, however, were not willing to believe that he had been blind and could now see, until they called the man's parents 19and asked them: "Is this your son? Do you say that he was born blind? Well, how is it that he can see now?" 20His parents answered: "We know that he is our son, and we know that he was born blind. 21But we do not know how it is that he is now able to see, nor do we know who opened his eyes. Ask him; he is old enough, and he can answer for himself!" 22His parents said this because they were afraid of the Jews; for the Jews had already agreed that if anyone professed that Jesus was the Messiah he would be put out of the synagogue. 23That is why his parents said, "He is old enough; ask him!"

24A second time they called back the man who had been born blind and said to him, "Promise before God that you will tell the truth! We know that this man is a sinner." 25"I do not know if he is a sinner or not," the man replied. "One thing I do know: I was blind, and now I see." 26"What did he do to you?" they asked. "How did he open your eyes?" 27"I have already told you," he answered, "and you would not listen. Why do you want to hear it again? Maybe you, too, would like to be his disciples?" 28They cursed him and said: "You are that fellow's disciple; we are Moses' disciples. 29We know that God spoke to Moses; as for that fellow, we do not even know where he comes from!" 30The man answered: "What a strange thing this is! You do not know where he comes from, but he opened my eyes! 31We know that God does not listen to sinners; he does listen to people who respect him and do what he wants them to do. 32Since the beginning of the world it has never been heard of that someone opened the eyes of a man born blind; 33unless this man came from God, he would not be able to do a thing." 34They answered back, "You were born and raised in sin—and you are trying to teach us?" And they threw him out of the synagogue.

35Jesus heard that they had thrown him out. He found him and said, "Do you believe in the Son of Man?" 36The man answered, "Tell me who he is, sir, so I can believe in him!" 37Jesus said to him, "You have already seen him, and he is the one who is talking with you now." 38"I believe, Lord!" the man said, and knelt down before Jesus.

In the story of the man born blind, the reader notes the contrast between Jesus' concern for the blind man and the callous unconcern of the Pharisees. The Pharisees, as the text makes clear, ignore Jesus' miraculous cure and concentrate legalistically on the fact that the cure took place on the Sabbath (9:13–16). They uncaringly **intimidate** the blind man's parents in hopes that the parents will confirm their own lack of belief in Jesus (9:17–23). They **turn a deaf ear** to all testimony in favor of Jesus' miracle. When all else fails, they try to discredit Jesus.

The contrast is even more striking when we see the Pharisees' on the one hand **expel** the blind man from their presence and on the other see Jesus **seek** him out and **offer** him, in addition to physical sight, the spiritual sight that comes from believing in the Son of Man. The difference between the blind man and the Pharisees is in their openness to the truth.

In this sequence John is out to emphasize the obstinate moral blindness of the Jewish leaders. Unlike the government official in sequence 8 (4:46–54), who believed without seeing, the Pharisees, with an abundance of firsthand evidence before their eyes, will neither see nor believe. They are closed to the truth.

Jesus' accusation that the Pharisees are blind sets the stage for the parable of the good shepherd (10:1–21).

Section Two (9:39—10:21)
Jesus Condemns the Pharisees as False Shepherds

[39]Jesus said, "I came to this world to judge, so that the blind should see, and those who see should become blind." [40]Some Pharisees, who were there with him, heard him say this and asked him, "You don't mean that we are blind, too?" [41]Jesus answered, "If you were blind, then you would not be guilty; but since you say, 'We can see,' that means that you are still guilty.

10 "I tell you the truth: the man who does not enter the sheepfold by the door, but climbs in some other way, is a thief and a robber. ²The man who goes in by the door is the shepherd of the sheep. ³The gatekeeper opens the gate for him; the sheep hear his voice as he calls his own sheep by name, and he leads them out. ⁴When he has brought them out, he goes ahead of them, and the sheep follow him, because they know his voice. ⁵They will not follow someone else; instead, they will run away from him, because they do not know his voice."

⁶Jesus told them this parable, but they did not understand what he was telling them.

⁷So Jesus said again: "I tell you the truth: I am the door for the sheep. ⁸All others who came before me are thieves and robbers; but the sheep did not listen to them. ⁹I am the door. Whoever comes in by me will be saved; he will come in and go out, and find pasture. ¹⁰The thief comes only in order to steal, kill, and destroy. I have come in order that they might have life, life in all its fullness. ¹¹I am the good shepherd. The good shepherd is willing to die for the sheep. ¹²The hired man, who is not a shepherd and does not own the sheep, leaves them and runs away when he sees a wolf coming; so the wolf snatches the sheep and scatters them. ¹³The hired man runs away because he is only a hired man and does not care for the sheep. ¹⁴ ¹⁵I am the good shepherd. As the Father knows me and I know the Father, in the same way I know my sheep and they know me. And I am willing to die for them. There are other sheep that belong to me that are not in this sheepfold. I must bring them, too; they will listen to my voice, and they will become one

flock with one shepherd. [17]The Father loves me because I am willing to give up my life, in order that I may receive it back again. [18]No one takes my life away from me. I give it up of my own free will. I have the right to give it, and I have the right to take it back. This is what my Father has commanded me to do."

[19]Again there was a division among the Jews because of these words. [20]Many of them were saying, "He has a demon! He is crazy! Why do you listen to him?" [21]But others were saying, "A man with a demon could not talk like this! How could a demon open the eyes of blind men?"

In this parable, Jesus describes his "work" in the world as that of the good shepherd, who, unlike the "bad" shepherds (the Pharisees), devotes his life to the care, protection, and salvation of his sheep. In view of what the reader has seen in the story of the man born blind, Jesus is certainly justified in condemning the Pharisees as bad shepherds.

The good shepherd parable makes excellent sense when one understands a few simple facts about the sheep pen, the gate, the gatekeeper, and the shepherds of Palestine in the first century. The sheep pen was a walled enclosure in which shepherds kept their flocks for safety overnight. The gatekeeper admitted the sheep to the pen and watched over them during the night. In the morning he would admit to the sheep pen only shepherds he recognized. Each shepherd would then call his sheep by name, much as a person calls his dog. The sheep, recognizing their own shepherd's voice, would follow him out of the sheep pen and be led to pasture, their shepherd walking in front of them.

The parable shows the Pharisees as false shepherds. They would **not** be admitted to the sheep pen by the gatekeeper, nor would the sheep recognize their **unfamiliar** voices. The only way for the false shepherds to get at the sheep would be the way of thieves and robbers, by going into the sheep pen over the wall.

■ *Reflection*
What are some forms of moral blindness which afflict people in our society today?

When Jesus tells the Pharisees this parable, they profess not to understand what he means. He explains the parable, therefore, and makes it more than obvious that the Pharisees are the thieves and robbers who only come in order to steal, kill, and destroy, whereas he alone is the good shepherd who cares for and protects the sheep and is even willing to die for them.

The parable thus carries over the contrast between Jesus' concern and the Pharisees' callous unconcern for the blind man in 9:1–38. It also carries over and continues the trial aspect of the whole of Part Four of the Gospel. In 9:16, the Pharisees, on the grounds that Jesus was not observing the Sabbath, reject his claim that he came from God. In 9:24, they accuse him of being a "sinner." Jesus counters these accusations in the good shepherd parable first, by solemnly declaring that he is from God because he does God's work (10:17–18) and second, by showing that he cured the blind man precisely because he is the *good shepherd* who cares for and loves his sheep. He loves them so much that he is even willing to die for them (10:11,18). No shepherd could do more!

■ *Reflection*

With the good shepherd parable fresh in your mind, read Psalm 23:1–6, the Lord is my shepherd.

■ Discussion

1. Outline a practical program for your parish to promote Christian unity so that there will be "one flock with one shepherd" (10:16).

2. How do the Gospel references to Abraham, Moses, and David illustrate that Jesus' new covenant is to replace the old covenant?

3. In what sense should our celebration of the Eucharist be a thanksgiving event?

4. Read "The Good Shepherd" in Ezekiel 34:11–31. How is this passage like the good shepherd parable in John 10:7–21? How is it different?

■ Prayer and Meditation

"But he spoke to the sky above
and commanded its doors to open;
he gave them grain from heaven,
by sending down manna for them to eat.
So they ate the food of angels,
and God gave them all they wanted."

Psalm 78:23–25

"Your ancestors ate manna in the desert, but they died. But the bread that comes down from heaven is of such a kind that whoever eats it will not die. I am the living bread that came down from heaven."

John 6:49–51a

Part Four (continuation) Controversy About Jesus' Credentials ____ John 10:22—12:11

This session concludes the study of Part Four of the Gospel according to John by focusing on sequences 15 and 16 as shown on the chart on page 16.

Sequence 15 (10:22—39) Jesus at the Feast of the Dedication

The informal trial of Jesus continues in sequence 15 (10:22—39) as the Jews accuse Jesus of blasphemy. In a scene set in winter at the Festival of the Dedication of the Temple, they contend that Jesus is only a man and refuse to believe that he is the Son of God. In reply, Jesus urges them to consider the deeds he performs. If they will examine his deeds, they will see that the Father is in him and that he is in the Father! Jesus' plea, however, only angers them the more—so much so that once again they try to seize him (10:39).

Sequence 15 (10:22—39)

²²The time came to celebrate the Feast of Dedication in Jerusalem; it was winter. ²³Jesus was walking in Solomon's Porch in the Temple, ²⁴when the Jews gathered around him and said, "How long are you going to keep us in sus-

pense? Tell us the plain truth: are you the Messiah?''

[25]Jesus answered: "I have already told you, but you would not believe me. The works I do by my Father's authority speak on my behalf; [26]but you will not believe because you are not my sheep. [27]My sheep listen to my voice; I know them, and they follow me. [28]I give them eternal life, and they shall never die; and no one can snatch them away from me. [29]What my Father has given me is greater than all, and no one can snatch them away from the Father's care. [30]The Father and I are one.''

[31]Then the Jews once more picked up stones to throw at him.

[32]Jesus said to them, "I have done many good works before you which the Father gave me to do; for which one of these do you want to stone me?'' [33]The Jews answered back: "We do not want to stone you because of any good works, but because of the way in which you insult God! You are only a man, but you are trying to make yourself God!'' [34]Jesus answered: "It is written in your own Law that God said, 'You are gods.' [35]We know that what the scripture says is true forever; and God called them gods, those people to whom his message was given. [36]As for me, the Father chose me and sent me into the world. How, then, can you say that I insult God because I said that I am the Son of God? [37]Do not believe me, then, if I am not doing my Father's works. [38]But if I do them, even though you do not believe me, you should at least believe my works, in order that you may know once and for all that the Father is in me, and I am in the Father.''

[39]Once more they tried to arrest him, but he slipped out of their hands.

The heart of the argument in the sequence is reached when Jesus declares, "The Father and I are one" (10:30). In response, the Jews try to stone him for blasphemy because, as they say, "You are only a man, but you are trying to make yourself God!" In return, Jesus argues that since earthly judges to whom God's message was given can be called gods (as they are in Psalm 82:6), then with all the more reason can he be called God since he is the Son of God and the one the Father chose to send into the world (10:34–36). If the Jews will not believe his words, Jesus continues, they should at least believe his deeds. Then they would know that the Father is in him and that he is in the Father.

Sequence 15 concludes with the Jews still refusing to believe in Jesus and once more seeking to arrest him (10:39). So ends the last great confrontation between Jesus and the Jewish leaders. In sequence 16 which follows, the Jewish leaders will gather in private and plot the death of Jesus. Jesus' hour of glory is rapidly approaching.

As we conclude sequence 15, we see that its main themes are those of witness and response. Jesus witnesses to his messiahship and divinity, and the response of the Jews of Jerusalem is resoundingly negative.

Note that sequence 15 as well as sequence 13, which come on either side of the good shepherd parable, take place at Jewish festivals at which the Jews gathered to praise, honor, and worship God. Ironically, they reject God himself who is personally in their midst teaching in the Temple about himself, about his Father, and about eternal life, which he offers to them.

Looking back at sequences 13, 14, and 15, we can see that John designedly places the shepherd figure (10:1–21) at the center of Part Four in order to portray for his audience the contrast between Jesus, the good shepherd, and the uncaring hirelings of the synagogue. We must never lose sight of the fact, however, that John emphasizes the negative response of the Jewish leaders because he is writing for Jews who are constantly swayed by the arguments of the synagogue and as a consequence hesitate to make a firm decision in favor of Christ and Christianity. Thus the negative response of the Jewish leaders allows John to present his audience with a choice. They can either choose Jesus and a true spiritual life or choose the synagogue and a life of legalism.

■ Reflection
Take time to consider Christian living today as expressed in terms of both deeds and words.

Sequence 16 (10:40—12:11) Lazarus, the Priests' Plot, and the Anointing

In the first four sequences of Part Four of his Gospel, John has dramatized the theological dispute between Christianity and the synagogue and has emphasized the bad faith of the synagogue leaders. With sequence 16 (10:40—12:11), John concludes Part Four by dramatizing the raising of Lazarus, thus demonstrating Jesus' power over death and at the same time showing conclusively not only the Jewish leaders' willful blindness but also their malicious determination to get rid of Jesus by having him put to death. The sequence is long. John, therefore, breaks it down into five sections: the first (10:40—42) balancing with the last (12:10—11), the second (11:1—44) with the fourth (12:1—9), and the third (11:45—57) in the center. Careful attention to the parallel structure and to the theme of belief will help considerably toward understanding both John's purpose in this long sequence and his method of achieving his purpose:

Parallel Structure of Sequence 16

Section one: At Bethany beyond the Jordan, **many believe** in Jesus (10:40–42).

Section two: At Bethany near Jerusalem, Jesus raises **buried** Lazarus (11:1–44).

Section three: The Jewish leaders plot to kill Jesus because so many people are believing in him because of Lazarus (11:45–57).

Section four: At Bethany near Jerusalem, Mary anoints Jesus for **burial** (12:1–9).

Section five: At Bethany near Jerusalem, **many believe** in Jesus (12:10–11).

Sequence 16 (10:40—12:11)

⁴⁰Jesus went back again across the Jordan river to the place where John had been baptizing, and stayed there. ⁴¹Many people came to him. "John did no mighty works," they said, "but everything he said about this man was true." ⁴²And many people there believed in him.

11 A man named Lazarus, who lived in Bethany, became sick. Bethany was the town where Mary and her sister Martha lived. (²This Mary was the one who poured the perfume on the Lord's feet and wiped them with her hair; it was her brother Lazarus who was sick.) ³The sisters sent Jesus a message, "Lord, your dear friend is sick." ⁴When Jesus heard it he said, "The final result of this sickness will not be the death of Lazarus; this has happened to bring glory to God, and will be the means by which the Son of God will receive glory." ⁵Jesus loved Martha and her sister, and Lazarus. ⁶When he received the news that Lazarus

was sick, he stayed where he was for two more days. [7]Then he said to the disciples, "Let us go back to Judea." [8]"Teacher," the disciples answered, "just a short time ago the Jews wanted to stone you; and you plan to go back there?" [9]Jesus said: "A day has twelve hours, has it not? So if a man walks in broad daylight he does not stumble, because he sees the light of this world. [10]But if he walks during the night he stumbles, because there is no light in him." [11]Jesus said this, and then added. "Our friend Lazarus has fallen asleep, but I will go wake him up." [12]The disciples answered, "If he is asleep, Lord, he will get well." [13]But Jesus meant that Lazarus had died; they thought he meant natural sleep. [14]So Jesus told them plainly, "Lazarus is dead; [15]but for your sake I am glad that I was not with him, so you will believe. Let us go to him." [16]Thomas (called the Twin) said to his fellow disciples, "Let us all go along with the Teacher, that we may die with him!" [17]When Jesus arrived, he found that Lazarus had been buried four days before. [18]Bethany was less than two miles from Jerusalem, [19]and many Jews had come to see Martha and Mary to comfort them about their brother's death. [20]When Martha heard that Jesus was coming, she went out to meet him; but Mary stayed at home. [21]Martha said to Jesus, "If you had been here, Lord, my brother would not have died! [22]But I know that even now God will give you whatever you ask of him." [23]"Your brother will be raised to life," Jesus told her. [24]"I know," she replied, "that he will be raised to life on the last day." [25]Jesus said to her: "I am the resurrection and the life. Whoever believes in me will live, even though he dies; [26]and whoever lives and believes in me will never die. Do you believe this?" [27]"Yes, Lord!" she answered. "I do believe that you are the Messiah, the Son of God, who was to come into the world." ²⁸After Martha said this she went back and called her sister Mary privately. "The Teacher is here," she told her, "and is asking for you." ²⁹When Mary heard this she got up and hurried out to meet him. (³⁰Jesus had not arrived in the village yet, but was still in the place where Martha had met him.) ³¹The Jews who were in the house with Mary comforting her followed her when they saw her get up and hurry out. They thought that she was going to the grave, to weep there. ³²When Mary arrived where Jesus was and saw him, she fell at his feet. "Lord," she said, "if you had been here, my brother would not have died!" ³³Jesus saw her weeping, and the Jews who had come with her weeping also; his heart was touched, and he was deeply moved. ³⁴"Where have you buried him?" he asked them. "Come and see, Lord," they answered. ³⁵Jesus wept. ³⁶So the Jews said, "See how much he loved him!" ³⁷But some of them said, "He opened the blind man's eyes, didn't he? Could he not have kept Lazarus from dying?" ³⁸Deeply moved once more, Jesus went to the tomb, which was a cave with a stone placed at the entrance. ³⁹"Take the stone away!" Jesus ordered. Martha, the dead man's sister, answered, "There will be a bad smell, Lord. He has been buried four days!" ⁴⁰Jesus said to her, "Didn't I tell you that you would see God's glory if you believed?" ⁴¹They took the stone away. Jesus looked up and said: "I thank you, Father, that you listen to me. ⁴²I know that you always listen to me, but I say this because of the people here, so they will believe that you sent me." ⁴³After he had said this he called out in a loud voice, "Lazarus, come out!" ⁴⁴The dead man came out, his hands and feet wrapped in grave cloths, and a cloth around his face. "Untie him," Jesus told them, "and let him go."

⁴⁵Many of the Jews who had come to visit Mary saw what Jesus did, and believed in him. ⁴⁶But some of them returned to the Pharisees and told them what Jesus had done. ⁴⁷So the Pharisees and the chief priests met with the Council and said: "What shall we do? All the mighty works this man is doing! ⁴⁸If we let him go on in this way everyone will believe in him, and the Roman authorities will take action and destroy the Temple and our whole nation!" ⁴⁹One of them, named Caiaphas, who was High Priest that year, said: "You do not know a thing! ⁵⁰Don't you realize that it is better for you to have one man die for the people, instead of the whole nation being destroyed?" (⁵¹Actually, he did not say this of his own accord; rather, as he was High Priest that year, he was prophesying that Jesus was about to die for the Jewish people, ⁵²and not only for them, but also to bring together into one body all the scattered children of God.) ⁵³So from that day on the Jewish authorities made plans to kill Jesus. ⁵⁴Therefore Jesus did not travel openly in Judea, but left and went to a place near the desert, to a town named Ephraim, where he stayed with the disciples. ⁵⁵The Jewish Feast of Passover was near, and many people went up from the country to Jerusalem, to perform the ceremony of purification before the feast. ⁵⁶They were looking for Jesus, and as they gathered in the Temple they asked one another, "What do you think? Surely he will not come to the feast, will he?" ⁵⁷The chief priests and the Pharisees had given orders that if anyone knew where Jesus was he must report it, so they could arrest him.

12 Six days before the Passover, Jesus went to Bethany, where Lazarus lived, the man Jesus had raised from death. ²They had prepared a dinner for him there, and Martha helped serve it, while Lazarus sat at the table with Jesus. ³Then Mary took a whole pint of a very expensive perfume made of nard, poured it on Jesus' feet, and wiped them with her hair. The sweet smell of the perfume filled the whole house. ⁴One of Jesus' disciples, Judas Iscariot—the one who would betray him—said, ⁵"Why wasn't this perfume sold for three hundred dollars and the money given to the poor?" ⁶He said this, not because he cared for the poor, but because he was a thief; he carried the money bag and would help himself from it. ⁷But Jesus said: "Leave her alone! Let her keep what she has for the day of my burial. ⁸You will always have poor people with you, but I will not be with you always." ⁹A large crowd of the Jews heard that Jesus was in Bethany, so they went there; they went, not only because of Jesus, but also to see Lazarus, whom Jesus had raised from death.

¹⁰So the chief priests made plans to kill Lazarus too; ¹¹because on his account many Jews were leaving their leaders and believing in Jesus.

Section one begins with Jesus going "back across the river Jordan to the place where John had been baptizing." This place, as we know from 1:28, is "Bethany on the east side of the Jordan river," a place about ninety miles north of the Bethany near Jerusalem where Lazarus lived. The section ends with the words, "And **many** people there **believed in him.**" The words are significant because John concludes section five with a similar statement: "So the chief priests made plans to kill

Lazarus too, because on his account **many** Jews were rejecting them and **believing in Jesus.**"

These two passages, with their emphasis on **many** people who were **believing in Jesus,** form a framework around sequence 16 as a whole and provide the thematic thread that links all five sections, namely, the Jewish leaders' fear of Jesus because so many were coming to believe in him! John expresses this theme succinctly: "So the Pharisees and the chief priests met with the Council and said, 'What will we do? Look at all the miracles this man is performing! If we let him go on in this way, **everyone will believe in him,** and the Roman authorities will take action and destroy our Temple and our nation!'" (11:47–48). It should be noted in passing that the synoptic Gospels agree with John in attributing the plot against Jesus to the fear felt by the priests and the Pharisees when they realized that many of the people were beginning to believe in Jesus.

John's emphasis on the "many" that were believing in Jesus may seem strange. Until now, John showed divisions among the people. Some were inclined to accept him. Others rejected him. But now John is clearly demonstrating the real motive for the Jewish leaders' plot to kill Jesus—they fear their own loss of power, prestige, and authority. Such fear leads to desperation and desperate deeds!

Section two, the raising of Lazarus (11:1–44), is presented as the "final straw"—that event which incited the Jewish leaders to actively plot the death of Jesus (11:45–57).

John tells the story of the raising of Lazarus from the dead in a way different from the way he tells his other miracle stories. The Lazarus story is much longer and more detailed than the healing of the official's son

(4:45–54), the cure of the paralytic (5:1–18), the feeding of the five thousand (6:1–15), and the healing of the man born blind (9:1–38). John tells these miracle stories not so much to emphasize the miracles but rather to emphasize the lack of faith of those who witnessed them. In the raising of Lazarus, however, he focuses attention on the miracle itself. Everything in the story leads up to the climactic miracle of the resurrection of Lazarus from the dead.

John's purpose in the Lazarus story is to focus his audience's attention on Jesus' power to give **both** physical and eternal life. He goes to great lengths to leave no doubt that Lazarus was really dead. He notes specifically that when Jesus heard that Lazarus was ill, he delayed going to him for two days (11:6). When the disciples misunderstood Jesus' statement that Lazarus had "fallen asleep," John makes it clear that Jesus meant Lazarus was already dead (11:11–15). When Jesus finally arrives at Bethany, it is pointed out that Lazarus had been buried for four days (11:17). The observation is also made that **many** Judeans knew of Lazarus' death and had come to comfort Martha and Mary (11:19). It is noted that Martha, Mary, and others rebuked Jesus for not coming in time to save Lazarus from dying (11:21, 32,37). Finally, when Jesus asks for the stone to be removed, Martha reminds him once again that Lazarus has been buried for four days and there will be "a bad smell" (11:39), that is, Lazarus is expected to have begun to decompose.

John leaves no doubt in anyone's mind that Lazarus was as dead as he could be. John even observes that Lazarus came out of the tomb still entwined in his burial cloths!

Through this detailed story, John assures his audience that the raising of Lazarus was indeed an authentic miracle demanding superhuman power! It is true that Jesus showed his superhuman power by raising Lazarus to physical life. But Lazarus was raised from the dead to prove that Jesus also had the power to give eternal life **to those who believed in him!** (11:40–42). The dramatic aspects of the whole narrative, therefore, are meant to emphasize Jesus' power to give **eternal life** to those who believe. The promises made to Nicodemus (3:1–21), to the Samaritan woman (4:4–26), and to others have now been shown to be eminently believable.

Ironically, as we shall see in section three (11:45–57), it is because Jesus raises Lazarus from the dead, thus bringing many to believe in him, that the Pharisees and priests decide to put him to death. For John's Christian audience, there is the added irony that the Jewish leaders, who thought they were going to get rid of Jesus by having him put to death, were actually setting the scene for Jesus' own resurrection from the dead.

Section three, the priests' plot to kill Jesus (11:45–57), is in many ways the climax of the whole sequence. The action picks up, the tension mounts, the hour of decision is at hand! One must ask, "Could John have found a better way than this to underscore the blindness and hatred of the Jewish leaders?" Some people protect their authority at any price! A greater price than the death of the innocent cannot be imagined. It is no wonder that when Jesus stood before Pilate, he declared: "You have authority over me only because it was given you by God. So the man [the Jewish leaders] who handed me over to you is guilty of a worse sin."

The reader at this point should reflect on the deep theological implications of the words of Caiaphas, that "it is better for you to have one man die for the people, instead of having the whole nation destroyed" (11:50). Caiaphas unwittingly spoke the truth. Not only the Jewish "nation" but all humanity (11:51–52), through Christ's death, will be saved from destruction and brought back into the sheepfold of Christ.

Section four, the anointing of Jesus which foreshadows his burial (12:1–9), takes place in John's Gospel at a different time than in the Gospels according to Matthew and Mark. In Matthew and Mark, Jesus is anointed following his triumphant entry into Jerusalem and just prior to his betrayal by Judas (Matthew 26:6–13; Mark 14:3–9). But John places the anointing before these events. He does so for two reasons. First, it provides a perfect parallel with section two (11:1–44). There he had spoken about Mary and Martha, and about Lazarus' burial and resurrection at Bethany. Here in section four (12:1–9), the story returns again to the same place, the same friends, and the same theme of death and burial, and thus throws the reader's mind back to section two (11:1–44) and its message about death and resurrection.

Second, since the Pharisees and priests had already decided on Jesus' death (11:45–57), it is entirely fitting that, by directing attention to the anointing of Jesus for burial, John should begin immediately to focus his audience's attention on that death as the climax of the whole Gospel. Indeed, as John will show in Part Five of his Gospel, the hour of Jesus' death is the "hour" of his glory, the "hour" when he completes his "work" by fulfilling the will of his Father, who "loved the world so much that he gave his only Son, so that everyone who believes in him may not die but have eternal life" (3:16).

Section five (12:10–11) completes the whole sequence by returning to the theme of section one, namely, that many were believing in Jesus. Thus the sequence ends as it began, with many Jews from Bethany near Jerusalem believing in Jesus just as many from Bethany beyond the Jordan believed in him.

Sequence 16 brings to an end the trial motif of Part Four but continues the themes of witness and response. The reader sees Jesus witnessing to himself by raising Lazarus from the dead and Martha responding for herself and the "many" by declaring: "Yes, Lord! . . . I do believe that you are the Messiah, the Son of God, who was to come into the world" (11:27).

For John's audience, the raising of Lazarus proves the truth of Jesus' claim to have power to give new life. It should also demonstrate for his audience that even so momentous a miracle was not enough to open the willfully closed eyes of the Jewish leaders. Rather than rejoice in Jesus' power manifested in raising Lazarus, the Jewish leaders, fearful of losing their own power, prestige, and authority, preferred to deny Jesus and plot his death (11:45–57).

The scene is set, therefore, for Part Five of the Gospel, in which John gives his account of the arrival of Jesus' "hour" of glory—the hour of his passion, death, burial, and resurrection.

■ *Reflection*

Tell in your own words how the story of the raising of Lazarus affects your attitude toward death and dying.

Meditate for a few moments on Martha's response to Jesus (11:27), and then make your own prayerful faith response to him.

■ Discussion

1. Discuss the divinity of Jesus Christ as a key truth of our Christian faith.

2. What are some ways in which Christians sometimes choose a life of legalism over a true spiritual life?

3. Explain the annual observance of the feasts and seasons of the Christian liturgical year as both a way of worship and a means of instruction in faith.

■ Prayer and Meditation

"I felt the powerful presence of the LORD, and his spirit took me and set me down in a valley where the ground was covered with bones . . . . God said to me, 'Mortal man, the people of Israel are like these bones. They say that they are dried up, without any hope and with no future. So prophesy to my people Israel and tell them that I, the Sovereign LORD, am going to open their graves. . . . When I open the graves where my people are buried and bring them out, they will know that I am the LORD. I will put my breath in them, bring them back to life, and let them live in their own land.' "

Ezekiel 37:1,11–14

"LORD, I will live for you, for you alone;
Heal me and let me live.
My bitterness will turn into peace.
You save my life from all danger;
You forgive all my sins.
No one in the world of the dead can praise you;
The dead cannot trust in your faithfulness.
It is the living who praise you.
As I praise you now."

Isaiah 38:16–19

"Jesus said to [Martha], 'I am the resurrection and the life. Whoever believes in me will live, even though he dies; and whoever lives and believes in me will never die. Do you believe this?' "

John 11:25–26

Part Five Jesus' Entry into Jersualem and His Farewell Discourse —————— John 12:12—17:26

The last two sessions of this guide deal with Part Five of the Gospel according to John. Study Session Five covers Jesus' entry into Jerusalem and Jesus' long farewell discourse at the Last Supper. Study Session Six covers John's passion narrative and his account of Jesus' appearances to Mary Magdalene and to the apostles after the resurrection.

In his final part of the Gospel (12:12—21:25), John sums up his central themes and at the same time brings to a climax all the mysterious remarks he has made about the "work" of the Father, the "work" of the Son, and the "work" that pertains to his audience, to the Church, and to all humankind.

As we proceed, keep in mind the importance of such fundamental Johannine themes as witness, response, and replacement, as well as the meaning of such mysterious Johannine terms as "work," "hour," "glory," and "being lifted up." All these terms refer to the one crowning event in Jesus' life on earth—his passion, death, and return to the Father. In these sequences the "hour" is the hour of his death, the hour when he completes his "work" of giving his life to prove to the world his and his Father's love for all humankind. "Being lifted up" is John's way of speaking about Jesus' death on the cross as something glorious—as Jesus' way back to life and to the bosom of the Father (see 1:18). "Glory," as we will see, is the most difficult of these terms to understand. To John it means the union of the Father and the Son in mutual love, and it means the manifestation of this mutual love to the world through the obedience of the Son in going to the cross to demonstrate to the world the reality and intensity of this love for all humankind. John has much to say about Jesus' "glory" in the famous Last Supper discourse.

In addition, John has his usual five sequences in Part Five (see the chart on page 16). His arrangement of the sequences helps considerably toward understanding in depth the climactic conclusion of his Gospel:

17—Jesus comes to Jerusalem and his hour arrives (12:12–50).
18—Jesus gives his farewell discourse to the apostles at the Last Supper (chapters 13—17).
19—Jesus' passion, death, and burial (chapters 18—19).
20—Jesus appears to Mary Magdalene (20:1–18).
21—Jesus appears three times to his apostles (20:19–21:25).

Sequence 17 (12:12–50)
Jesus Comes to Jerusalem and His Hour Arrives

This first sequence of Part Five is the most difficult to understand. Fortunately, John divides it into five sections, with sections one and five and sections two and four in parallel, and with section three in the center. This division provides clues for interpreting the whole sequence.

Parallel Structure of Sequence 17

Section one: The crowd greets Jesus **as a nationalistic messiah** (12:12–19).

Section two: The Greeks **want to "see"** Jesus (12:20–22).

Section three: Jesus declares the "hour" has arrived for the salvation of the world (12:23–36).

Section four: The Jews **refuse to "see"** even though Jesus has done so many signs before them (12:37–43).

Section five: Jesus comes **as God's emissary**, sent by the Father to save the world (12:44–50).

Read the sequence first according to its parallel sections (one and five, then two and four) and then read it as a whole from beginning to end. After a careful reading, try to see it as a whole according to its five-section parallel structure.

Sequence 17 (12:12—50)

¹²The next day the large crowd that had come to the Passover Feast heard that Jesus was coming to Jerusalem. ¹³So they took branches from palm trees and went out to meet him, shouting: "Praise God! God bless him who comes in the name of the Lord! God bless the King of Israel!" ¹⁴Jesus found a donkey and sat on it, just as the scripture says: ¹⁵"Do not be afraid, city of Zion! Now your King is coming to you, Riding a young donkey." ¹⁶His disciples did not understand this at the time; but when Jesus had been raised to glory they remembered that the scripture said this, and that they had done this for him. ¹⁷The crowd that had been with Jesus when he called Lazarus out of the grave and raised him from death had reported what had happened. ¹⁸That was why the crowd met him—because they heard that he had done this mighty work. ¹⁹The Phari-

sees then said to each other, "You see, we are not succeeding at all! Look, the whole world is following him!"

²⁰Some Greeks were among those who went to Jerusalem to worship during the feast. ²¹They came to Philip (he was from Bethsaida, in Galilee) and said, "Sir, we want to see Jesus." ²²Philip went and told Andrew, and the two of them went and told Jesus.

²³Jesus answered them: "The hour has now come for the Son of Man to be given great glory. ²⁴I tell you the truth: a grain of wheat is no more than a single grain unless it is dropped into the ground and dies. If it does die, then it produces many grains. ²⁵Whoever loves his own life will lose it; whoever hates his own life in this world will keep it for life eternal. ²⁶Whoever wants to serve me must follow me, so that my servant will be with me where I am. My Father will honor him who serves me. ²⁷Now my heart is troubled—and what shall I say? Shall I say, 'Father, do not let this hour come upon me'? But that is why I came, to go through this hour of suffering. ²⁸O Father, bring glory to your name!" Then a voice spoke from heaven, "I have brought glory to it, and I will do so again." ²⁹The crowd standing there heard the voice and said, "It thundered!" Others said, "An angel spoke to him!" ³⁰But Jesus said to them: "It was not for my sake that this voice spoke, but for yours. ³¹Now is the time for the world to be judged; now the ruler of this world will be overthrown. ³²When I am lifted up from the earth, I will draw all men to me." (³³In saying this he indicated the kind of death he was going to suffer.) ³⁴The crowd answered back: "Our Law tells us that the Messiah will live forever. How, then, can you say that the Son of

Man must be lifted up? Who is this Son of Man?" ³⁵Jesus answered: "The light will be among you a little longer. Live your lives while you have the light, so the darkness will not come upon you; because the one who lives in the dark does not know where he is going. ³⁶Believe in the light, then, while you have it, so that you will be the people of the light." After Jesus said this he went off and hid himself from them.

³⁷Even though he had done all these mighty works before their very eyes they did not believe in him, ³⁸so that what the prophet Isaiah had said might come true: "Lord, who believed the message we told? To whom did the Lord show his power?" ³⁹For this reason they were not able to believe, because Isaiah also said: ⁴⁰"God has blinded their eyes, He has closed their minds, So that their eyes would not see, Their minds would not understand, And they would not turn to me For me to heal them." ⁴¹Isaiah said this because he saw Jesus' glory, and spoke about him. ⁴²Even then, many Jewish leaders believed in Jesus; but because of the Pharisees they did not talk about it openly, so as not to be put out of the synagogue. ⁴³They loved the approval of men rather than the approval of God.

⁴⁴Jesus spoke in a loud voice: "Whoever believes in me, believes not only in me but also in him who sent me. ⁴⁵Whoever sees me, also sees him who sent me. ⁴⁶I have come into the world as light, that everyone who believes in me should not remain in the darkness. ⁴⁷Whoever hears my message and does not obey it, I will not judge him. I came, not to judge the world, but to save it. ⁴⁸Whoever rejects me and does not accept my message, has one who will judge him. The word I have spoken will be his judge

on the last day! ⁴⁹Yes, because I have not spoken on my own, but the Father who sent me
has commanded me what I must say and
speak. ⁵⁰And I know that his command brings
eternal life. What I say, then, is what the Father has told me to say.''

The first clue to the interpretation of 12:12–50 is provided by the contrast between section one and section
five. In section one (12:12–19), Jesus purposely enters
Jerusalem humbly and on a donkey as predicted by the
prophet Zechariah (see Zechariah 9:9). He thus
manifests his objection to the crowd's intent to welcome him as a nationalistic, power-politics messiah. He
had objected and fled to the hills alone when the Jews
of Galilee attempted to make him king following his
multiplication of the loaves (6:14–15). In section five
(12:44–50), which parallels section one, Jesus declares
the true nature of his messiahship: he has come ''into
the world as light, so that everyone who believes in me
should not remain in darkness.'' He claims that he
speaks not on his own authority but on the authority of
the Father who sent him and has commanded him
what he must say and speak (12:49). In short, he has not
come as a power-politics messiah but as the emissary of
the Father, sent by the Father to save the world by
bringing to eternal life those who believe in him (12:50).
Later on, before Pilate, he will declare unambiguously,
''My kingdom does not belong to this world'' (18:36).

The second clue is provided by the contrast
between the Greeks in section two (12:20–22) who **want
to "see,"** that is, who want to believe in Jesus, and the
Jews in section four (12:37–43) who **refuse to "see"** and
believe even though Jesus had performed so many miracles in their presence.

Earlier in the Gospel, the evangelist alluded to the universality of Jesus' mission. John the Baptist pointed to Jesus as "the Lamb of God who takes away the sin of the world" (1:29). Jesus had declared that "God so loved the world that he gave his only Son" (3:16). The Samaritans called Jesus "the Savior of the world" (4:42). In these passages, John was anticipating Jesus' mission to the **world**, his gathering of the other sheep into the one fold (10:16), and his in-gathering through his death of all the scattered children of God (11:52).

The fact that John says so little about the incident with the Greeks and that Jesus does not even speak to them is significant. It demonstrates the evangelist's purely symbolic purpose in incorporating this otherwise strange and abruptly dismissed episode. It is understandable when one recalls that John's Gospel is written for Jewish Christians on the fence between Christianity and the synagogue. If he had written his Gospel for a gentile audience, we may be sure he would have said a great deal more about the Greeks. Here, however, he simply wants to **contrast** once more the blindness of the Jewish leaders with the openness of those who **want** to see, that is, those who want to believe in Jesus.

The third and most important clue to sequence 17 is found in section three (12:23–36). Immediately following the coming of the Greeks, Jesus solemnly declares: "The hour has now come for the Son of Man to receive great glory." In the earlier parts of the Gospel, all we had heard were Jesus' mysterious statements that his "hour" **had not yet come** (see 2:5; 7:6; 7:30; 8:20). That this mysterious "hour" is the "hour" of Jesus' death is now made clear! The little parable of the grain of wheat which **must die** before it can produce fruit (12:24) expresses the meaning of Jesus' "hour." It is even further clarified by

Jesus' words about being "lifted up from the earth" in 12:32–34.

If one studies section three in relationship to sections one, two, four, and five, one can see that it contains the most important clue of all for the interpretation of the whole of sequence 17 precisely because it makes perfectly clear that Jesus is a **suffering** Messiah and not the kind of power-politics messiah the Jews wanted when they cheered Jesus entering Jerusalem during the Passover Festival (12:12–19). The truth that it is God's will that Jesus be a **suffering** Messiah is borne out by Jesus' prayer, "Father, bring glory to your name," and the Father's immediate response to his prayer, "I have brought glory to it, and I will do so again."

Sequence 17, with its theme of suffering and dying, introduces the climactic fifth part of John's Gospel and thereby sets the stage for both Jesus' farewell discourse in chapters 13—17 and for the passion and resurrection narratives in chapters 18—21.

■ *Reflection*

Recall an "hour" of decision or crisis in your own life. What was the outcome? How did it affect you and others?

Sequence 18 (13:1—17:26)
Jesus' Farewell Discourse

John's account of Jesus' farewell discourse calls for long and deeply meditative reading. Too much commentary can spoil it. It is meant to be mulled over, savored, made one's own in the stillness of meditation. We give here, therefore, only the clues which we consider indispensable to a fruitful reading of this great discourse.

The first clue is to read the discourse **as a farewell discourse**. It is the night before Jesus' death. Jesus knows he will soon die. He knows that his absence, while in the tomb and after his return to the Father following the resurrection, will create a void in the life of his disciples. He knows his disciples need encouragement, hope, and instruction on how to follow him and continue his work. He knows his last words will be remembered, repeated, and treasured. He will speak, therefore, about the significance of his death, about the consolations he has in store for his followers, about the Holy Spirit who will be with them, and about the necessity of their union with him, as the branch with the vine, if they are to bear fruit.

The second clue is to read the discourse as the medium John has chosen through which to present Jesus' teaching on discipleship. As noted earlier, all four Gospels follow a basic format: first, Jesus' credentials; second, response to Jesus' credentials; third, instructions on discipleship; fourth, Jesus' passion, death, and resurrection. In John's Gospel, almost everything John says about discipleship is put into the farewell discourse. In reading the discourse, therefore, one should repeatedly ask: "What is Jesus saying to the apostles and to all Christians about following him?"

For this second clue, however, one must place oneself in the shoes of the apostles, feel the poignancy of Jesus' sadness, and experience the bewilderment of the apostles as they realize that Jesus is really going to die. Now finally they understand the great mission Jesus has entrusted to them as well as the wonderful words of consolation he expresses.

The third clue is to read the discourse according to John's five section format and thus see it as a whole.

Section one (13:1–32) provides the introduction to the discourse. It shows how Jesus, loving his own "to the very end," uses the footwashing to symbolize his death for others and to teach his apostles how far their love for others is to go. Judas' betrayal then signals the hour of Jesus' death and glorification.

Sequence 18 (Chapters 13—17)

Section One (13:1–32)
The Footwashing and
Judas the Traitor

13 It was now the day before the Feast of Passover. Jesus knew that his hour had come for him to leave this world and go to the Father. He had always loved those who were his own in the world, and he loved them to the very end.

²Jesus and his disciples were at supper. The Devil had already decided that Judas, the son of Simon Iscariot, would betray Jesus. ³Jesus knew that the Father had given him complete power; he knew that he had come from God and was going to God. ⁴So Jesus rose from the table, took off his outer garment, and tied a towel around his waist. ⁵Then he poured some water into a washbasin and began to wash the disciples' feet and dry them with the towel around his waist. ⁶He came to Simon Peter, who said to him, "Are you going to wash my feet, Lord?" ⁷Jesus answered him, "You do not know now what I am doing, but you will know later." ⁸Peter declared, "You will never, at any time, wash my feet!" "If I do not wash your feet," Jesus answered, "you will no longer be my disciple." ⁹Simon Peter answered, "Lord, do not wash only my feet, then! Wash

my hands and head, too!" ¹⁰Jesus said: "Whoever has taken a bath is completely clean and does not have to wash himself, except for his feet. All of you are clean—all except one." (¹¹Jesus already knew who was going to betray him; that is why he said, "All of you, except one, are clean.")

¹²After he had washed their feet, Jesus put his outer garment back on and returned to his place at the table. "Do you understand what I have just done to you?" he asked. ¹³"You call me Teacher and Lord, and it is right that you do so, because I am. ¹⁴I am your Lord and Teacher, and I have just washed your feet. You, then, should wash each other's feet. ¹⁵I have set an example for you, so that you will do just what I have done for you. ¹⁶I tell you the truth: no slave is greater than his master; no messenger is greater than the one who sent him. ¹⁷Now you know this truth; how happy you will be if you put it into practice!

¹⁸"I am not talking about all of you; I know those I have chosen. But the scripture must come true that says, 'The man who ate my food turned against me.' ¹⁹I tell you this now before it happens, so that when it does happen you will believe that 'I Am Who I Am.' ²⁰I tell you the truth: whoever receives anyone I send, receives me also; and whoever receives me, receives him who sent me." ²¹After Jesus said this, he was deeply troubled, and declared openly: "I tell you the truth: one of you is going to betray me." ²²The disciples looked at one another, completely puzzled about whom he meant. ²³One of the disciples, whom Jesus loved, was sitting next to Jesus. ²⁴Simon Peter motioned to him and said, "Ask him who it is that he is talking about." ²⁵So that disciple moved closer to Jesus' side and asked, "Who is

it, Lord?" ²⁶Jesus answered, "I will dip the bread in the sauce and give it to him; he is the man." So he took a piece of bread, dipped it, and gave it to Judas, the son of Simon Iscariot. ²⁷As soon as Judas took the bread, Satan went into him. Jesus said to him, "Hurry and do what you must!"

(²⁸None of those at the table understood what Jesus said to him. ²⁹Since Judas was in charge of the money bag, some of the disciples thought that Jesus had told him to go to buy what they needed for the feast, or else that he had told him to give something to the poor.) ³⁰Judas accepted the bread and went out at once. It was night. ³¹After Judas had left, Jesus said: "Now the Son of Man's glory is revealed; now God's glory is revealed through him. ³²And if God's glory is revealed through him, then God himself will reveal the glory of the Son of Man, and he will do so at once."

Scholars are agreed that the washing of the feet symbolizes Jesus' death. To make sure this symbolism is understood, John clues in his audience by telling them that "Jesus knew that the hour had come for him to **leave this world** and go to the Father" and that Jesus "had always loved those in the world who were his own, and he loved them **to the very end**" (that is, as much as it is possible to love). Later, Jesus says the same thing in these words: "The greatest love a person can have for his friends is to give his life for them" (15:13).

John clues in his audience even better by having Peter misunderstand Jesus. Peter objects because he thinks Jesus is humiliating himself by washing his feet (13:6–8). Jesus corrects him by saying, "You do not understand **now** what I am doing, but you will understand **later**." Later, after Jesus death, Peter will understand that Jesus' act of washing the feet of his disciples was meant to symbolize his death and thereby prove his love for his own "to the very end" (13:7).

It is only in the light of the washing as symbolic of his death and of his love to the end that Jesus' first words about discipleship can be fully grasped. In 13:15–17, he says, "I have set an example for you, so that you will do [for one another] **just what I have done for you** . . . how happy you will be if you put it into practice!" True disciples who follow Jesus' example will be willing to die for each other and will be happy when they do so!

Few Christians are called upon to actually die for others. But there are other ways of giving oneself for others. Giving one's time, attention, help, and goods is a way of dying for others. Such "giving" prepares the way for giving oneself "to the very end."

■ *Reflection*
Meditate on practical expressions of "giving oneself for others" in your own day-to-day following of Jesus.

Section two (13:33—14:31) begins the actual discourse as Jesus explains how the gap occasioned by his departure is to be filled.

Section Two (13:33—14:31)
Jesus Begins His Farewell Discourse

³³"My children, I shall not be with you very much longer. You will look for me; but I tell you now what I told the Jews, 'You cannot go where I am going.' ³⁴A new commandment I give you: love one another. As I have loved you, so you must love one another. ³⁵If you have love for one another, then all will know that you are my disciples." ³⁶"Where are you going, Lord?"

Simon Peter asked him. "You cannot follow me now where I am going," answered Jesus; "but later you will follow me." ³⁷"Lord, why can't I follow you now?" asked Peter. "I am ready to die for you!" ³⁸Jesus answered: "Are you really ready to die for me? I tell you the truth: before the rooster crows you will say three times that you do not know me.

14 Do not be worried and upset," Jesus told them. "Believe in God, and believe also in me. ²There are many rooms in my Father's house, and I am going to prepare a place for you. I would not tell you this if it were not so. ³And after I go and prepare a place for you, I will come back and take you to myself, so that you will be where I am. ⁴You know how to get to the place where I am going."

⁵Thomas said to him, "Lord, we do not know where you are going; so how can we know the way to get there?" ⁶Jesus answered him: "I am the way, I am the truth, I am the life; no one goes to the Father except by me. ⁷Now that you have known me," he said to them, "you will know my Father also; and from now on you do know him, and you have seen him." ⁸Philip said to him, "Lord, show us the Father; that is all we need." ⁹Jesus answered: "For a long time I have been with you all; yet you do not know me, Philip? Whoever has seen me has seen the Father. Why, then, do you say, 'Show us the Father'? ¹⁰Do you not believe, Philip, that I am in the Father and the Father is in me? The words that I have spoken to you," Jesus said to his disciples, "do not come from me. The Father, who remains in me, does his own works. ¹¹Believe me that I am in the Father and the Father is in me. If not, believe because of these works. ¹²I tell you the truth: whoever believes in me will do the works

I do—yes, he will do even greater ones, for I am going to the Father. [13]And I will do whatever you ask for in my name, so that the Father's glory will be shown through the Son. [14]If you ask me for anything in my name, I will do it.

[15]"If you love me, you will obey my commandments. [16]I will ask the Father, and he will give you another Helper, the Spirit of truth, to stay with you forever. [17]The world cannot receive him, because it cannot see him or know him. But you know him, for he remains with you and lives in you.

[18]"I will not leave you alone; I will come back to you. [19]In a little while the world will see me no more, but you will see me; and because I live, you also will live. [20]When that day comes, you will know that I am in my Father, and that you are in me, just as I am in you.

[21]"Whoever accepts my commandments and obeys them, he is the one who loves me. My Father will love him who loves me; I too will love him and reveal myself to him." [22]Judas (not Judas Iscariot) said, "Lord, how can it be that you will reveal yourself to us and not to the world?" [23]Jesus answered him: "Whoever loves me will obey my message. My Father will love him, and my Father and I will come to him and live with him. [24]Whoever does not love me does not obey my words. The message you have heard is not mine, but comes from the Father, who sent me. [25]I have told you this while I am still with you. [26]The Helper, the Holy Spirit whom the Father will send in my name, will teach you everything, and make you remember all that I have told you. [27]Peace I leave with you; my own peace I give you. I do not give it to you as the world does. Do not be worried and upset; do not be

afraid. [28]You heard me say to you, 'I am leaving, but I will come back to you.' If you loved me, you would be glad that I am going to the Father, because he is greater than I. [29]I have told you this now, before it all happens, so that when it does happen you will believe. [30]I cannot talk with you much longer, for the ruler of this world is coming. He has no power over me, [31]but the world must know that I love the Father; that is why I do everything as he commands me. Rise, let us go from this place.''

The discourse opens with a reference to Jesus' death: "My children, I will not be with you very much longer." It follows with the "new" commandment: " . . . love one another. As I have loved you, so you must love one another. If you have love for one another, then everyone will know that you are my disciples."

The "new" commandment seems to be introduced rather abruptly, until we realize that it has already been explained by the symbolism of the washing of the feet. The commandment to "love one another as I have loved you" is "new" because it calls upon people to die for one another as Jesus died for them. The old commandment, "Love your neighbor as yourself," never went that far, nor did it have Jesus' example of such love.

These first words of Jesus' farewell discourse say much about the **essence** of Christian discipleship. Christians who understand the essence of discipleship will always know how to answer Jesus' question to Peter in 13:38: "Are you **really** ready to die for me?"

In 14:1–31, Jesus makes a number of promises which provide encouragement and consolation to his apostles. These promises deal with preparation of "rooms in my Father's house" (14:2), doing what Jesus does (14:12), answering the prayers of his followers (14:13–14), and sending "another Helper," the Holy Spirit, to reveal to them "the truth about God" (14:15–17, 25–26). Jesus promises to return to his disciples (14:18–20), and finally he gives them the gift of his peace which is unlike anything the world can give (14:27).

Section three (15:1–25) explains how, during the time of the gap caused by Jesus' absence, the disciples must remain in Jesus as the branch remains in the vine.

Section Three (15:1–25)
The True Vine and the False Vine

15 "I am the real vine, and my Father is the gardener. ²He breaks off every branch in me that does not bear fruit, and prunes every branch that does bear fruit, so that it will be clean and bear more fruit. ³You have been made clean already by the message I have spoken to you. ⁴Remain in union with me, and I will remain in union with you. Unless you remain in me you cannot bear fruit, just as a branch cannot bear fruit unless it remains in the vine. ⁵I am the vine, you are the branches. Whoever remains in me, and I in him, will bear much fruit; for you can do nothing without me. ⁶Whoever does not remain in me is thrown out, like a branch, and dries up; such branches are gathered up and thrown into the fire, where they are burned.

⁷"If you remain in me, and my words remain in you, then you will ask for anything you wish, and you shall have it. ⁸This is how my Father's glory is shown: by your bearing much fruit; and in this way you become my

disciples. [9]I love you just as the Father loves me; remain in my love. [10]If you obey my commands, you will remain in my love, in the same way that I have obeyed my Father's commands and remain in his love.

[11]"I have told you this so that my joy may be in you, and that your joy may be complete.

[12]"This is my commandment: love one another, just as I love you. [13]The greatest love a man can have for his friends is to give his life for them. [14]And you are my friends, if you do what I command. [15]I do not call you servants any longer, because a servant does not know what his master is doing. Instead, I call you friends, because I have told you everything I heard from my Father. [16]You did not choose me; I chose you, and appointed you to go and bear much fruit, the kind of fruit that endures. And the Father will give you whatever you ask of him in my name. [17]This, then, is what I command you: love one another."

[18]"If the world hates you, you must remember that it has hated me first. [19]If you belonged to the world, then the world would love you as its own. But I chose you from this world, and you do not belong to it; this is why the world hates you. [20]Remember what I told you: 'No slave is greater than his master.' If they persecuted me, they will persecute you too; if they obeyed my message, they will obey yours too. [21]But they will do all this to you because you are mine; for they do not know him who sent me. [22]They would not have been guilty of sin if I had not come and spoken to them; as it is, they no longer have any excuse for their sin. [23]Whoever hates me hates my Father also. [24]They would not have been guilty of sin if I had not done the works among them that no one else

ever did; as it is, they have seen what I did and they hate both me and my Father. [25]This must be, however, so that what is written in their Law may come true, 'They hated me for no reason at all.' "

The beautiful parable of the vine and the branches deals with the necessity of union with Jesus if a person is to bear fruit. The parable is practically self-explanatory except for its teaching on discipleship, which is not always appreciated. Discipleship consists in a great deal more than simply believing in Jesus. It consists in doing what Jesus does, loving others, denying oneself for others, even dying for others. In the light of what Jesus says about his "new" commandment and about the sign by which "everyone will know that you [Christians] are my disciples" (13:34–35), it is easy to understand that Jesus refers to denying oneself for others even unto death when he says his Father "breaks off every branch in me [the real vine] that does not bear fruit, and he prunes every branch that does bear fruit, so that it will be clean and bear more fruit" (15:1–2). In short, the branches (disciples) who bear no fruit at all, that is, those who do not perform acts of love of neighbor, are cut away completely from the vine (see 15:6), while even those who do bear fruit are pruned (in the sense of "cut back," to insure greater growth) by hardships and persecution so that they will bear even more fruit (see 15:18–25). Union with Jesus the vine involves a union in love, and that love calls for the self-denying love of others.

Jesus underscores the lesson of the image of the vine and the branches by repeating in 15:11–17 the new commandment: "love one another, just as I love you." Jesus then describes the way he loves: "The greatest love a person can have for his friends is to give his life for them."

Section three ends with Jesus' prediction of what form the "pruning" of the disciples will take (15:18–25). They will be persecuted by the Jews as Jesus was persecuted. Jesus thus makes clear that he is the "true" vine, and the synagogue is the "false" vine, and that the Christian Church is the true Israel and the synagogue is the false Israel. There is no place in the kingdom of God for those who hate. God is love, and all in God's kingdom, symbolized by the vine, love as God loves and as Jesus loves!

Section four (15:26—16:33) concludes the discourse. It explains how in time of persecution Christians will have the assistance of the Helper, the Holy Spirit, to guide and console them in their witness to Jesus. They are also told that whatever they "ask in Jesus' name," they will receive. Finally, Jesus promises them his marvelous gift of peace.

Section Four (15:26—16:33)
Jesus Concludes
His Farewell Discourse

²⁶"The Helper will come—the Spirit of truth, who comes from the Father. I will send him from the Father, and he will speak about me. ²⁷And you, too, will speak about me, for you have been with me from the very beginning.

16 I have told you this so that you will not fall away. ²They will put you out of their synagogues. And the time will come when anyone who kills you will think that by doing this he is serving God. ³They will do these things to you because they have not known either the Father or me. ⁴But I have told you this, so that when the time comes for them to do these things, you will remember that I told you. I did not tell you these things at the beginning, because I was with you.

⁵"But now I am going to him who sent me; but none of you asks me, 'Where are you going?' ⁶And now that I have told you, sadness has filled your hearts. ⁷But I tell you the truth: it is better for you that I go away, because if I do not go, the Helper will not come to you. But if I do go away, then I will send him to you. ⁸And when he comes he will prove to the people of the world that they are wrong about sin, and about what is right, and about God's judgment. ⁹They are wrong about sin, because they do not believe in me; ¹⁰about what is right, because I am going to the Father and you will not see me any more; ¹¹about judgment, because the ruler of this world has already been judged. ¹²I have much more to tell you, but now it would be too much for you to bear. ¹³But when the Spirit of truth comes, he will lead you into all the truth. He will not speak on his own, but he will tell you what he hears, and will speak of things to come. ¹⁴He will give me glory, for he will take what I have to say and tell it to you. ¹⁵All that my Father has is mine; that is why I said that the Spirit will take what I give him and tell it to you.

¹⁶"In a little while you will not see me any more; and then a little while later you will see me." ¹⁷Some of his disciples said to the others: "What does this mean? He tells us, 'In a little while you will not see me, and then a little while later you will see me'; and he also says, 'It is because I am going to the Father.' ¹⁸What does this 'a little while' mean?" they asked. "We do not know what he is talking about!" ¹⁹Jesus knew that they wanted to ask him, so

he said to them: "I said, 'In a little while you will not see me, and then a little while later you will see me.' Is this what you are asking about among yourselves? [20]I tell you the truth: you will cry and weep, but the world will be glad; you will be sad, but your sadness will turn into gladness. [21]When a woman is about to give birth to a child she is sad, because her hour of suffering has come; but when the child is born she forgets her suffering, because she is happy that a baby has been born into the world. [22]That is the way it is with you: now you are sad, but I will see you again, and your hearts will be filled with gladness, the kind of gladness that no one can take away from you.

[23]"When that day comes you will not ask me for a thing. I tell you the truth: the Father will give you anything you ask of him in my name. [24]Until now you have not asked for anything in my name; ask and you will receive, so that your happiness may be complete. [25]I have told you these things by means of parables. But the time will come when I will use parables no more, but I will speak to you in plain words about the Father. [26]When that day comes you will ask him in my name; and I do not say that I will ask him on your behalf, [27]for the Father himself loves you. He loves you because you love me and have believed that I came from God. [28]I did come from the Father and I came into the world; and now I am leaving the world and going to the Father." [29]Then his disciples said to him: "Look, you are speaking very plainly now, without using parables. [30]We know now that you know everything; you do not need someone to ask you questions. This makes us believe that you came from God."

[31]Jesus answered them: "Do you believe now? [32]The time is coming, and is already here,

when all of you will be scattered, each one to his own home, and I will be left all alone. But I am not really alone, because the Father is with me. [33]I have told you this so that you will have peace through your union with me. The world will make you suffer. But be brave! I have defeated the world!"

Jesus promises the help of the Holy Spirit because he knows his followers will be persecuted (16:1–4). With the help of the Holy Spirit, he assures them they will see their persecutors proved wrong and themselves led to and kept in the truth (16:4b–15).

The reference to expulsion from the synagogues in 16:2 probably alludes to excommunication from the synagogue. There is good evidence that about the year 85 A.D. the Pharisees convened a synod at Jamnia and decreed that Jews who became Christians were to be expelled from the synagogue. This decree was no small matter for Christian Jews. It meant not only exclusion from the synagogue but also exclusion from the community in which they lived and socialized. In many cases, such an exclusion meant separation from family, loss of job, and even physical punishment. There is no evidence that the synagogue authorities actually had Christian Jews put to death, but the experience of Saint Paul, who was frequently scourged, indicates less lethal punishments were not unusual. All in all, a Jew who became a Christian did so at great sacrifice. Under such circumstances, it is understandable that Jesus should go out of his way both to warn his followers and at the same time to try to encourage and console them.

In the remainder of section four, Jesus repeats much that he said in section two (13:33—14:31) about his going away, about the sending of the Holy Spirit, about their not seeing him for a little while and then seeing him a little while later, about answering their prayers, and about his gift of peace. All these things are repeated now in the context of Jesus' warnings about persecutions to come. It is in view of such persecutions that Jesus now prays for his apostles and his Church.

Section five (17:1–26) contains Jesus' prayer to his Father for his apostles and for all those who believe in him.

Section Five (17:1–26)
Jesus Prays for the Church

17 After Jesus finished saying this, he looked up to heaven and said: "Father, the hour has come. Give glory to your Son, that the Son may give glory to you. ²For you gave him authority over all men, so that he might give eternal life to all those you gave him. ³And this is eternal life: for men to know you, the only true God, and to know Jesus Christ, whom you sent. ⁴I showed your glory on earth; I finished the work you gave me to do. ⁵O Father! Give me glory in your presence now, the same glory I had with you before the world was made.

⁶"I have made you known to the men you gave me out of the world. They belonged to you, and you gave them to me. They have obeyed your word, ⁷and now they know that everything you gave me comes from you. ⁸For I gave them the message that you gave me, and they received it; they know that it is true that I came from you, and they believe that you sent me.

⁹"I pray for them. I do not pray for the world, but for the men you gave me, because

they belong to you. ¹⁰All I have is yours, and all you have is mine; and my glory is shown through them. ¹¹And now I am coming to you; I am no longer in the world, but they are in the world. O holy Father! Keep them safe by the power of your name, the name you gave me, so they may be one just as you and I are one. ¹²While I was with them I kept them safe by the power of your name, the name you gave me. I protected them, and not one of them was lost, except the man who was bound to be lost— that the scripture might come true. ¹³And now I am coming to you, and I say these things in the world so that they might have my joy in their hearts, in all its fullness.

¹⁴"I gave them your message and the world hated them, because they do not belong to the world, just as I do not belong to the world. ¹⁵I do not ask you to take them out of the world, but I do ask you to keep them safe from the Evil One. ¹⁶Just as I do not belong to the world, they do not belong to the world. ¹⁷Make them your own, by means of the truth; your word is truth. ¹⁸I sent them into the world just as you sent me into the world. ¹⁹And for their sake I give myself to you, in order that they, too, may truly belong to you.

²⁰"I do not pray only for them, but also for those who believe in me because of their message. ²¹I pray that they may all be one. O Father! May they be in us, just as you are in me and I am in you. May they be one, so that the world will believe that you sent me. ²²I gave them the same glory you gave me, so that they may be one, just as you and I are one: ²³I in them and you in me, so they may be completely one, in order that the world may know that you sent me and that you love them as you love me. ²⁴O Father! You have given them to me, and I

want them to be with me where I am, so they may see my glory, the glory you gave me; for you loved me before the world was made. [25]O righteous Father! The world does not know you, but I know you, and these know that you sent me. [26]I made you known to them and I will continue to do so, in order that the love you have for me may be in them, and I may be in them."

The actual farewell discourse, as we have seen, begins at 13:33 and ends at 16:33. In section five, Jesus no longer speaks to his disciples but directs himself in prayer to his Father. It is important to note that this prayer is a prayer not only for the Church at the time when the Gospel was written but for the Church of all times. The key concept of the prayer is the concept we have seen Jesus emphasize throughout the Gospel— the concept of "work": Jesus' work, the work of the apostles, and the work of the Church. The prayer is uttered at the Last Supper, but the Jesus who prays it is no longer of this world. He projects into the future his death and resurrection and speaks, as it were, from beyond the grave to Christians of all times. This is obvious from 17:4 where Jesus says, "I have finished the work you gave me to do." The "work" is Jesus' passion and death, the subject matter of chapters 18 and 19 in the Gospel of John.

When Jesus prays for his apostles (17:9–19) but not for the "world," he is praying for the success of the apostles' "work," which like his own is to bring people to faith in him and thus to eternal life. Here, therefore, the word "world" does not refer to humanity in general as it does in 1:29, 3:16, and 4:42 but to the "world" as that group in humanity which opposes the salvific work of Jesus. In the context of the whole discourse, the group about which Jesus speaks is the synagogue (see 15:18–16:4). For John's Jewish Christian audience, the "world" that opposes the work of Jesus is the "world" of the synagogue!

Jesus prays also "for those who believe in me because of the apostles' message" (17:20–26). His prayer is for all the millions of Christians down through the centuries who through the preaching of the apostles and their successors have come to believe in him. For them, too, there will be, not necessarily persecution, but certainly difficulties in living up to Jesus' new commandment: "As I have loved you, so you must love one another" (13:34).

Jesus' special prayer for all Christians is "that they may all be one" (17:21). Keeping in mind what Jesus says about loving his apostles "to the very end" (13:1), about his "new commandment" (13:34–35), and about the "greatest love a person can have for his friends" (15:13–14), it is easy to deduce that it is self-sacrificing love for others that makes "all be one" in Jesus and in the Father. The Father loves the Son. The Son loves and dies for his people. His people love and die for one another. Thus all are one in love!

Jesus prays, "I gave them the same glory you gave me, so that they may be one, just as you and I are one" (17:22). By these words Jesus means that when people truly love "to the very end," they share in that mutual love which constitutes the glorious union of the Son and the Father. Then Jesus says, "Father! You have given them to me, and I want them to be with me where I am, so that they may see my glory, the glory you gave me: for you loved me before the world was made" (17:24). Here he refers to the ultimate union of his followers with him in heaven. There they will witness the everlasting union and mutual love of the Father and the Son.

Christians who have understood the farewell discourse, and especially Jesus' prayer for the apostles and for the Church (17:1–26), will have gone a long way toward understanding not only what Jesus means by love "to the very end" (13:1) but also what he means by his words, "I have set an example for you" (13:15) and "If you have love for one another, then everyone will know that you are my disciples" (13:15). We all become "one" (17:21) when we love one another as the Father loves Jesus, as Jesus loves the Father, and as the Father and the Son love each of us. The "indwelling" about which Jesus speaks in 17:22–23 is an indwelling in mutual love. It is the heart of the Trinity. It is the goal of a true Christian's life. Christian discipleship, in short, is summed up in the words, "If you have love for one another, then everyone will know that you are my disciples" (13:35). It is a difficult but convincing test!

■ *Reflection*

Tell in your own way just what it means to you to "follow" Jesus.

What difficulties do you experience in living up to Jesus' new commandment? How do you cope with such difficulties?

■ Discussion

1. The Church is one, holy, catholic, apostolic. What insights into these characteristics have you gained from your study of the Gospel according to John?

2. At the Last Supper Jesus gave his apostles and his Church the gift of the Eucharist. In what sense is the Eucharist the great sacred sign of unity and peace for Christians?

3. Discuss the ten commandments in light of Jesus' new commandment.

4. In what practical way can Christians be instruments for peace—family, community, nation, world?

■ Prayer and Meditation

"The new covenant that I will make with the people of Israel will be this: I will put my law within them and write it on their hearts. I will be their God, and they will be my people."

Jeremiah 31:33

"And now I give you a new commandment: love one another. As I have loved you, so you must love one another. If you have love for one another, then everyone will know that you are my disciples."

John 13:34–35

Part Five (continuation) Jesus' Passion, Death, and Resurrection —— John 18:1—21:25

Study Session Six, the last session in this program, continues and concludes the presentation of the Gospel according to John. It covers the final sequences (19, 20, 21) of Part Five as shown on the chart on page 16.

Sequence 19 (18:1—19:42) Jesus' Passion, Death, and Burial

John's passion account (18:1—19:42), beginning with Jesus' arrest in the garden, is substantially the same as the passion narratives of Matthew (26:36—27:66), Mark (14:32—15:47), and Luke (22:47—23:56). All four evangelists divide the account into the same five parts: the arrest; the trial before the high priest; the trial before Pilate; the crucifixion; the burial. We say "substantially" the same, because while all four evangelists speak about the same events, there are notable differences in the way John tells the story from the way Matthew, Mark, and Luke tell it.

John views the whole of the passion as the climactic fulfillment of Jesus' "work." For John, it is the "hour" of Jesus' glory, when Jesus does the will of his Father, "who loved the world so much that he **gave** his only Son"

(3:16). It is the "hour" of triumph when Jesus is "lifted up from the earth" and draws "everyone" to himself (12:32). It is the "hour" of Jesus' exaltation! John divides his passion account into the following five sections:

Parallel Structure of Sequence 19

Section one: Arrested in a **garden,** Jesus is **bound** and led away to trial (18:1–12).

Section two: Jesus, **the true high priest,** is put on trial before Caiaphas. The **"beloved disciple"** is present (18:13–27).

Section three: Jesus, the King of Israel, is judged by Pilate and rejected by his own people (18:28—19:16).

Section four: As **true high priest,** Jesus, like Isaac, carries the wood of his own sacrifice. The **"beloved disciple"** is present (19:17–30).

Section five: **Bound** with burial cloths, Jesus is buried in a **garden** (19:31–42).

John's view of the passion as Jesus' hour of exaltation helps to explain why John eliminates or adds to certain words and events found in the basic passion narratives of Matthew, Mark, and Luke. It also explains why he emphasizes theological teachings not emphasized by them. These distinct variations are particularly noticeable in section one, the account of Jesus' arrest in the garden.

Section one (18:1–12) is notable primarily for John's omission of the famous agony in the garden and Judas' kiss of betrayal. Instead John emphasizes Jesus' willingness to complete the work his Father gave him.

Section One (18:1—12)
Jesus' Arrest

18 After Jesus had said this prayer he left with his disciples and went across the brook Kidron. There was a garden in that place, and Jesus and his disciples went in. ²Judas, the traitor, knew where it was, because many times Jesus had met there with his disciples. ³So Judas went to the garden, taking with him a group of soldiers and some Temple guards sent by the chief priests and the Pharisees; they were armed and carried lanterns and torches.

⁴Jesus knew everything that was going to happen to him; so he stepped forward and said to them, "Who is it you are looking for?" ⁵"Jesus of Nazareth," they answered. "I am he," he said. Judas, the traitor, was standing there with them.

⁶When Jesus said to them, "I am he," they moved back and fell to the ground.

⁷Jesus asked them again, "Who is it you are looking for?" "Jesus of Nazareth," they said. ⁸"I have already told you that I am he," Jesus said. "If, then, you are looking for me, let these others go." (⁹He said this so that what he had said might come true: "Not a single one was lost, Father, of all those you gave me.")

¹⁰Simon Peter had a sword; he drew it and struck the High Priest's slave, cutting off his right ear. The name of the slave was Malchus. ¹¹Jesus said to Peter, "Put your sword back in its place! Do you think that I will not drink the

cup of suffering my Father has given me?"
[12] The group of soldiers with their commanding officer and the Jewish guards arrested Jesus, tied him up,

John eliminates Jesus' agony in the garden because he views the passion as the "hour" of Jesus' exaltation and glorification rather than as the time of Jesus' fearsome anguish and suffering. He eliminates Judas' kiss of betrayal because for John it is Jesus, not the traitor, who initiates the fateful hour of the passion. This view fits in with Jesus' words at the end of the good shepherd parable: "No one takes my life away from me. I give it up of my own free will" (10:18).

Jesus' threefold repetition of the words "I am he" (in 18:5,6,8) reminds the reader once more of what Jesus said to the Pharisees in 8:56: "Before Abraham was born, **'I Am' "** (8:56). The words "I am" or "I am he" in John's Gospel always allude to the name God gave himself when Moses asked him his name and he replied by saying, "I am who I am" (Exodus 3:14). The soldiers' reaction in 18:6: "They drew back and fell to the ground," is another way John chooses to emphasize Jesus' divine nature. His Jewish Christian audience would readily recognize here a reference to Psalm 27:2, in which the psalmist says of his enemies, "When evil men attack me and try to kill me, they stumble and **fall**."

The final Johannine touch in the arrest scene is found in 18:11 when Peter raises his sword to defend Jesus and Jesus says to him, "Put your sword back in its place! Do you think that I will not drink the cup of suffering which my Father has given me?" John has eliminated the story of the agony in the garden, but he does not eliminate its central point. Jesus' reference to "the cup of suffering which my Father has given me" would remind the reader that in Mark's account of the agony Jesus had said, "Take this cup of suffering away from me. Yet not what I want, but what you want" (Mark 14:36). They would remind the reader also of what Jesus said about his "work" in John 4:34: "My food . . . is to obey the will of the one who sent me and to finish the work he gave me to do." In what follows, we shall see Jesus more than ready to finish the work his Father gave him to do.

Section two (18:13–27) presents the trial scene before the high priest and is notable for the little John says about the trial and the great deal he says about Peter's denial of Jesus.

Section Two (18:13–27)
Jesus' Trial and Peter's Denial

¹³and took him first to Annas. He was the father-in-law of Caiaphas, who was High Priest that year. ¹⁴It was Caiaphas who had advised the Jews that it was better that one man die for all the people. ¹⁵Simon Peter and another disciple followed Jesus. That other disciple was well known to the High Priest, so he went with Jesus into the courtyard of the High Priest's house. ¹⁶Peter stayed outside by the gate. The other disciple, who was well known to the High Priest, went back out, spoke to the girl at the gate and brought Peter inside. ¹⁷The girl at the gate said to Peter, "Aren't you one of the disciples of that man?" "No, I am not," answered Peter. ¹⁸It was cold, so the servants and guards had built a charcoal fire and were standing around it, warming themselves. Peter went over and stood with them, warming himself.

¹⁹The High Priest questioned Jesus about his disciples and about his teaching.

²⁰Jesus answered: "I have always spoken publicly to everyone; all my teaching was done in the synagogues and in the Temple, where all the Jews come together. I have never said anything in secret.

²¹"Why, then, do you question me? Question the people who heard me. Ask them what I told them—they know what I said." ²²When Jesus said this, one of the guards there slapped him and said, "How dare you talk like this to the High Priest!" ²³Jesus answered him: "If I have said something wrong, tell everyone here what it was. But if I am right in what I have said, why do you hit me?"

²⁴So Annas sent him, still tied up, to Caiaphas the High Priest. ²⁵Peter was still standing there keeping himself warm. So the others said to him, "Aren't you one of the disciples of that man?" But Peter denied it. "No, I am not," he said. ²⁶One of the High Priest's slaves, a relative of the man whose ear Peter had cut off, spoke up. "Didn't I see you with him in the garden?" he asked. ²⁷Again Peter said "No"—and at once a rooster crowed.

In section two, the only thing John says about the trial is that Annas questioned Jesus and then sent him to Caiaphas. Almost everything else deals with Peter's threefold denial of Jesus (18:15–18, 25–27). It is particularly noticeable that John eliminates from his account of the trial the question put to Jesus by Caiaphas in Matthew 26:63: "In the name of the living God I now put you under oath: tell us if you are the Messiah, the Son of God." The simplest explanation of such a skimpy trial account is that John had already summarized the results of the trial in 11:45–52. There, following the raising of Lazarus, John explained how the Sanhedrin, led by

Caiaphas, met and condemned Jesus to death. For the same reason, he finds it equally unnecessary to include the condemnation of Jesus by the Sanhedrin as recorded in the synoptic Gospels: "What do you think?" [asked the high priest]. They answered, "He is guilty and must die" (Matthew 26:66).

With no need to recount the details of the trial, John uses the trial scene to focus attention on Jesus' prediction in 13:38 that Peter would deny him: "Before the rooster crows you will say three times that you do not know me." It is precisely these three denials on which John focuses. The first denial takes place when the girl at the gate questions Peter; the second, when the group at the charcoal fire questions him; the third, when a slave of the high priest questions him. John makes sure his audience remembers Jesus' prediction of Peter's denials by commenting after the third denial, "and at once a rooster crowed."

One might ask, "Why place so much emphasis on the fulfillment of Jesus' prophecy concerning Peter's threefold denial?" The answer would be that John emphasizes the fulfillment of Jesus' prophecy in order to make it clear that Jesus, rather than either Annas or Caiaphas, is the true prophet and the true high priest of Israel.

Section three (18:28—19:16a) contains John's account of Jesus' trial before Pilate. It emphasizes three points: first, the nature of Jesus' kingdom; second, the innocence of Jesus; and third, the guilt of Pilate and the Jewish leaders. The Gospel of John presents the trial before Pilate in seven scenes alternating between outside and inside the praetorium.

²⁸They took Jesus from Caiaphas' house to the Governor's palace. It was early in the morning. The Jews did not go inside the palace because they wanted to keep themselves ritually clean, in order to be able to eat the Passover meal. ²⁹So Pilate went outside to meet them and said, "What do you accuse this man of?" ³⁰Their answer was, "We would not have brought him to you if he had not committed a crime." ³¹Pilate said to them, "You yourselves take him and try him according to your own law." The Jews replied, "We are not allowed to put anyone to death." (³²This happened to make come true what Jesus had said when he indicated the kind of death he would die.)

³³Pilate went back into the palace and called Jesus. "Are you the king of the Jews?" he asked him. ³⁴Jesus answered, "Does this question come from you or have others told you about me?" ³⁵Pilate replied: "Do you think I am a Jew? It was your own people and their chief priests who handed you over to me. What have you done?" ³⁶Jesus said: "My kingdom does not belong to this world; if my kingdom belonged to this world, my followers would fight to keep me from being handed over to the Jews. No, my kingdom does not belong here!" ³⁷So Pilate asked him, "Are you a king, then?" Jesus answered: "You say that I am a king. I was born and came into the world for this one purpose, to speak about the truth. Whoever belongs to the truth listens to me." ³⁸"And what is truth?" Pilate asked.

Then Pilate went back outside to the Jews and said to them: "I cannot find any reason to condemn him. [39]But according to the custom you have, I always set free a prisoner for you during the Passover. Do you want me to set the king of the Jews free for you?" [40]They answered him with a shout, "No, not him! We want Barabbas!" (Barabbas was a bandit.)

19 Then Pilate took Jesus and had him whipped. [2]The soldiers made a crown of thorny branches and put it on his head; they put a purple robe on him, [3]and came to him and said, "Long live the King of the Jews!" And they went up and slapped him.

[4]Pilate went back out once more and said to the crowd, "Look, I will bring him out here to you, to let you see that I cannot find any reason to condemn him." [5]So Jesus went outside, wearing the crown of thorns and the purple robe. Pilate said to them, "Look! Here is the man!" [6]When the chief priests and the guards saw him they shouted, "Nail him to the cross! Nail him to the cross!" Pilate said to them, "You take him, then, and nail him to the cross. I find no reason to condemn him." [7]The Jews answered back, "We have a law that says he ought to die, because he claimed to be the Son of God." [8]When Pilate heard them say this, he was even more afraid.

[9]He went back into the palace and said to Jesus, "Where do you come from?" But Jesus gave him no answer. [10]Pilate said to him, "You will not speak to me? Remember, I have the authority to set you free, and also the authority to have you nailed to the cross." [11]Jesus answered, "You have authority over me only because it was given to you by God. So the man who handed me over to you is guilty of a worse sin."

¹²When Pilate heard this he was all the more anxious to set him free. But the Jews shouted back, "If you set him free that means you are not the Emperor's friend! Anyone who claims to be a king is the Emperor's enemy!" ¹³When Pilate heard these words, he took Jesus outside and sat down on the judge's seat in the place called "The Stone Pavement." (In Hebrew the name is "Gabbatha.") ¹⁴It was then almost noon of the day before the Passover. Pilate said to the Jews, "Here is your king!" ¹⁵They shouted back, "Kill him! Kill him! Nail him to the cross!" Pilate asked them, "Do you want me to nail your king to the cross?" The chief priests answered, "The only king we have is the Emperor!" ¹⁶Then Pilate handed Jesus over to them to be nailed to the cross.

In the first scene, **outside** the praetorium, the trial begins with the Jewish leaders trying to persuade Pilate to condemn Jesus to death. In the second scene, *inside* the praetorium, Pilate engages Jesus in a discussion about kingship. Characteristically, Jesus declares, "My kingdom does not belong to this world." What is notable about Jesus' statement is its consistency. In 6:14–15, when the Galilean Jews wanted to make him a power-politics messianic king, he rebuked them by fleeing to the mountains. In 12:12–19, when the Jews of Jerusalem greeted him on Palm Sunday as a nationalistic messianic king, he protested their misunderstanding of the nature of his kingship by riding into Jerusalem on a donkey, thus signifying that he came as a humble Messiah and not as a power-politics, world-conquering messiah. From the beginning to the end of his Gospel, John insists on the spiritual nature of Jesus' kingship and kingdom!

This first discussion with Pilate concludes with a touch of Johannine irony. Pilate asks, "And what is truth?" The irony, as John's audience would see it, lies in Pilate's asking such a question with Jesus, the answer to his question, standing directly in front of him!

In the third scene, Pilate is again **outside** with the Jews. He declares Jesus innocent: "I cannot find any reason to condemn him." But in complete contradiction to his judgment of innocence, he now puts Jesus on the same level as the condemned criminal Barabbas and allows the Jewish leaders to choose between Barabbas and Jesus. Given the choice, the Jews choose Barabbas.

The choice emphasizes the guilt of the Jewish leaders. It also serves to underline the irony of the situation for John and his audience. In Aramaic, the name Barabbas means "son of the father." Given the choice between the false "son of the father" and the true "Son of the Father," the Jews reject the true and elect the false. They have, of course, been rejecting the true Son of the Father throughout the Gospel. Such consistency on their part deserves no praise. They are as guilty as Pilate.

In scene four (19:1–3), Pilate compounds his guilt. Despite declaring, "I cannot find any reason to condemn him," Pilate hands over Jesus to be scourged. The scene is loaded with Johannine irony. John shows the soldiers inside the praetorium mocking Jesus by dressing him in royal purple and crowning him with a crown of thorns. They are trying to express what they think is ironic about the whole situation. The man, they propose, claims to be a king; then let him be clothed and crowned as if he were a king.

For John's audience, the scene is infused with a double irony. Jesus, whom the soldiers treat ironically as if he were a king, is, ironically, truly a king! Considering this scene, along with scene two where Pilate discusses the nature of Jesus' kingship and with scene six (19:9–11) where Pilate discusses with Jesus the nature of true authority, it is certain that John is using the trial before Pilate to instruct his audience on the true nature and the divine origin of Jesus' messiahship and authority.

In scene five (19:4–8), once again **outside** the praetorium, Pilate twice more repeats, "I cannot find any reason to condemn him." In hopes, however, of arousing the compassion of the crowd, Pilate presents Jesus, streaming with blood from the scourging and from the crowning with thorns, and says to the crowd, "Look! Here is the man!" When the Jews press for cruci-fixion, Pilate again compounds his own guilt by reply-ing, "You take him, then, and crucify him. I find no rea-son to condemn him." Here, once more, John emphasizes not only the guilt of the Jewish leaders but the guilt of Pilate as well. And, once more, John indulges in irony. Pilate says, "Look! Here is **the man!**" But John and his audience know that if Pilate had known Jesus' true identity, he would have said, "Look! Here is **the Son of God!**"

In scene six (19:9–11), back *inside* the praetorium, Pilate engages in a discussion with Jesus about the nature of authority. As in scene two, where Jesus declares his kingdom did not belong "to this world," so here he declares that Pilate has authority over him "only because it was given to [him] by God." Jesus' last words to Pilate, "So the man who handed me over to you is guilty of a worse sin," condemn Pilate but at the same time soften the condemnation. Those who handed Jesus over to Pilate are guilty of a worse sin.

Theoretically, Jesus could be referring to Judas. However, we must take into consideration what John says about the Jewish authorities and their demand for Jesus' death (18:28–32; 19:14–16) as well as what he has been saying about the Jewish leaders throughout the Gospel (see 5:15–18; 8:48–59; 11:45–54). In light of these passages, it is much more likely that Jesus is speaking about the Jews and using Judas as the representative of all those who have rejected him.

The trial ends in scene seven (19:12–16), once again **outside** the praetorium, with the Jews threatening Pilate, "If you set him free, that means you are not the Emperor's friend." Pilate stubbornly declares, "Here is your king." The Jews respond, "The only king we have is the Emperor." The whole scene is unutterably sad. Pilate, who has three times declared Jesus innocent, capitulates before the threats of the Jews. The Jews who have been awaiting their Messiah for a thousand years, declare, "The only king we have is the Emperor." They then see their true messianic king handed over to be crucified! The trial is over. The guilty have been judged by Jesus, the true judge of all the world. But the innocent one himself has been condemned to a frightful death on a cross.

■ *Reflection*
What are some Jesus-or-Barabbas choices that often confront today's society?

Section four (19:16b–30) gives John's account of the crucifixion. It is majestic, highly symbolic, and extraordinarily brief. It has only fourteen verses.

Section Four (19:16b–30)
Jesus' Death

So they took charge of Jesus. [17] He went out, carrying his own cross, and came to "The Place of the Skull," as it is called. (In Hebrew it is called "Golgotha.")

[18] There they nailed him to the cross; they also nailed two other men to crosses, one on each side, with Jesus between them.

[19] Pilate wrote a notice and had it put on the cross. "Jesus of Nazareth, the King of the Jews," is what he wrote. [20] Many Jews read this, because the place where Jesus was nailed to the cross was not far from the city. The notice was written in Hebrew, Latin, and Greek. [21] The Jewish chief priests said to Pilate, "Do not write 'The King of the Jews,' but rather, 'This man said, I am the King of the Jews.'" [22] Pilate answered, "What I have written stays written."

[23] After the soldiers had nailed Jesus to the cross, they took his clothes and divided them into four parts, one part for each soldier. They also took the robe, which was made of one piece of woven cloth, without any seams in it. [24] The soldiers said to each other, "Let us not tear it; let me throw dice to see who will get it." This happened to make the scripture come true: "They divided my clothes among themselves, They gambled for my robe." So the soldiers did this.

[25] Standing close to Jesus' cross were his mother, his mother's sister, Mary the wife of Clopas, and Mary Magdalene. [26] Jesus saw his mother and the disciple he loved standing there; so he said to his mother, "Woman, here is your son." [27] Then he said to the disciple,

"Here is your mother." And from that time the disciple took her to live in his home. [28]Jesus knew that by now everything had been completed; and in order to make the scripture come true he said, "I am thirsty." [29]A bowl was there, full of cheap wine; they soaked a sponge in the wine, put it on a branch of hyssop, and lifted it up to his lips. [30]Jesus took the wine and said, "It is finished!" Then he bowed his head and died.

The beginning of the account recalls the sacrifice of Isaac (Genesis 22:6). Like Isaac, the only beloved son of Abraham, Jesus carries the wood of his own sacrifice (19:17). Since Jesus will sacrifice himself on the cross, the symbolism of Isaac insinuates that Jesus is the true high priest of Israel and that his beloved Father is involved in the sacrifice. There are echoes here of Jesus' own words, "For God loved the world so much that he **gave** his only Son" (3:16), and, "No one takes my life away from me. I give it up of my own free will. I have the right to give it up, and I have the right to take it back. This is what my Father has commanded me to do" (10:18).

Readers have noticed that Simon of Cyrene, who helped Jesus carry his cross (see Mark 15:21), is eliminated from John's passion account. John eliminates him, we believe, in order to emphasize that Jesus needed no help in bringing about the redemption of the world.

The two criminals crucified with Jesus are mentioned because John needs them later in the passion narrative to make a point about Jesus' legs not being broken. The royal title on the cross is mentioned in order to link the crucifixion with John's emphasis in the trial before Pilate on Jesus' divine kingship (see 18:28—19:16). Jesus is crucified as a king!

The division of Jesus' garments among the soldiers focuses the reader's attention on Jesus' robe, "which was made of one piece of woven cloth without any seams in it" (19:23). Since such a garment "without any seams in it" was worn only by the high priest (see Leviticus 16:4), it seems likely that John mentions it to emphasize once more that Jesus is the true high priest of Israel and that his death on the cross represents the Passover sacrifice of the "Lamb of God, who takes away the sin of the world" (see 1:29 and 19:33–36).

Jesus' words to his mother and to the "beloved disciple" (19:26–27) most likely record Jesus' concern for his mother. Some interpreters, however, see Mary as symbolic of Judaism and the "beloved disciple" as symbolic of Christianity. If the evangelist sees them in this way, then by the words, "He is your son . . . . She is your mother," he wants to symbolize the unity of the old and the new Israel—a unity which in his own time he saw crumbling as a result of the synagogue's opposition to Christ and the Christian Church.

Finally, John's remark that Jesus says, "I am thirsty," contains an allusion to the words of Psalm 69:21: "when I was thirsty, they offered me vinegar." He makes the remark for two reasons. First, it reminds his audience of what Philip had said at the beginning of the Gospel: "We have found the one whom Moses wrote about in the book of the Law and whom the prophets also wrote about" (1:45). Thus these words point out that Jesus is the fulfillment of the Old Testament prophecies. Second, it focuses attention on Jesus' "work" by observing that after taking the vinegar, Jesus solemnly declares, "It is finished!" The "it" is Jesus' "work," of which he has stated: "My food . . . is to do the will of the one who sent me and **to finish the work he gave me to do**" (4:34). When Jesus dies, he has finished the work of redemption for which the Father sent him into the world.

Section five (19:31–42) gives John's account of the burial of Jesus. In this section he draws a parallel between the end and the beginning of his passion narrative.

Section Five (19:31–42)
Jesus' Burial

³¹Then the Jews asked Pilate to allow them to break the legs of the men who had been put to death, and take them down from the crosses. They did this because it was Friday, and they did not want the bodies to stay on the crosses on the Sabbath day, since the coming Sabbath was especially holy.

³²So the soldiers went and broke the legs of the first man and then of the other man who had been put to death with Jesus. ³³But when they came to Jesus they saw that he was already dead, so they did not break his legs. ³⁴One of the soldiers, however, plunged his spear into Jesus' side, and at once blood and water poured out.

³⁵The one who saw this happen has spoken of it. We know that what he said is true, and he also knows that he speaks the truth, so that you also may believe.

³⁶This was done to make the scripture come true, "Not one of his bones will be broken." ³⁷And there is another scripture that says, "People will look at him whom they pierced."

³⁸After this, Joseph, who was from the town of Arimathea, asked Pilate if he could take Jesus' body. (Joseph was a follower of Jesus, but in secret, because he was afraid of the Jews.) Pilate told him he could have the body, so Joseph went and took it away. ³⁹Nicodemus,

who at first had gone to see Jesus at night, went with Joseph, taking with him about one hundred pounds of spices, a mixture of myrrh and aloes. ⁴⁰The two men took Jesus' body and wrapped it in linen cloths with the spices; for this is how the Jews prepare a body for burial. ⁴¹There was a garden in the place where Jesus had been put to death, and in it there was a new tomb where no one had ever been laid. ⁴²Since it was the day before the Jewish Sabbath, and because the tomb was close by, they laid Jesus there.

In section one (18:1–12) John told how Jesus had been arrested **in a garden** and his hands had been **bound**. Now at the end of his passion account, John tells how Jesus' body is **bound** and placed in a new tomb **in a garden** (19:40–41). It is another brilliant example of John's use of the technique known as inclusion-conclusion, that is, ending with words that throw the reader's mind back to the beginning.

More important, however, John uses his account of the burial to focus attention on the fulfillment of Scripture and on Jesus as the Passover Lamb who takes away the sin of the world. As John notes, the soldiers **did not break** the legs of Jesus (19:32), thereby fulfilling the old covenant regulation that none of the Passover lamb's bones be broken (Exodus 12:46). Thus Jesus, who sacrificed himself on the cross, is seen by John to be the sacrificial Lamb of the new Passover and the new covenant!

The passion is over, but the story is not. There remains the resurrection, the appearance to Mary Magdalene, and the three appearances to the disciples. It is to these appearances that we now turn as we approach the end of John's Gospel.

Sequence 20 (20:1–18)
Mary at the Tomb

Gospel accounts of the resurrection concentrate on the empty tomb and on Jesus' appearances to different people after his resurrection. All four Gospels mention the empty tomb (Matthew 28:1–11; Mark 16:1–8; Luke 24:1–7; John 20:1–18). Three mention appearances of Jesus. None, however, describes the actual resurrection—the transition of Jesus from death to life. This silence, of course, is entirely fitting, since no one actually saw Jesus rise. They saw his empty tomb, and then they saw him in the flesh after the resurrection. The appearances and the empty tomb, therefore, emphasize the **fact** but not the **manner** of the resurrection, and they do so in different ways. John emphasizes the fact of the resurrection when he speaks about three appearances of Jesus in Jerusalem and one in Galilee; Luke, when he speaks about appearances to the disciples at Emmaus, to Peter, and later to all the apostles in Jerusalem (Luke 24); Matthew, when he speaks about one appearance in Jerusalem and one in Galilee (Matthew 28). Mark mentions no appearances at all but only the words of the angel: "He is going to Galilee ahead of you; there you will see him, just as he told you" (Mark 16:7).

These differences may seem strange, but contemporary readers should remember that the evangelists wrote their Gospels to give their own inspired interpretations of Jesus and of the events that took place in Jesus' life. They had no intention of writing full-scale biographies. Nor did they intend to give detailed historical descriptions of all the events of Jesus' life. They selected stories from the many traditions that came down to them and used those selected stories to convey their own inspired theological interpretations of Jesus and the events of his life.

We should not be surprised, therefore, that Mark has no resurrection appearance; Matthew, two; Luke, three; and John, four. Nor should we be surprised at so many different stories. The excitement that pervaded Easter morning and the rest of the day must have been immense. Out of such excitement, different stories were bound to arise. Each evangelist had his own reasons for selecting the particular traditional stories he needed to round out his inspired theological interpretation of Jesus.

In John's case, the story of Jesus' appearance to Mary Magdalene (sequence 20, as shown in the chart on page 16) is told to explain John's theology concerning faith and the resurrection (20:1–18).

Sequence 20 (20:1–18)

20 Early on Sunday morning, while it was still dark, Mary Magdalene went to the tomb and saw that the stone had been taken away from the entrance.

²She ran and went to Simon Peter and the other disciple, whom Jesus loved, and told them, "They have taken the Lord from the tomb and we don't know where they have put him!"

³Then Peter and the other disciple left and went to the tomb. ⁴The two of them were running, but the other disciple ran faster than Peter and reached the tomb first. ⁵He bent over and saw the linen cloths, but he did not go in. ⁶Behind him came Simon Peter, and he went straight into the tomb. He saw linen cloths lying there ⁷and the cloth which had been around

Jesus' head. It was not lying with the linen cloths but was rolled up by itself. [8]Then the other disciple, who had reached the tomb first, also went in; he saw and believed. ([9]They still did not understand the scripture which said that he must be raised from death.) [10]Then the disciples went back home.

[11]Mary stood crying outside the tomb. Still crying, she bent over and looked in the tomb, [12]and saw two angels there, dressed in white, sitting where the body of Jesus had been, one at the head, and the other at the feet. [13]"Woman, why are you crying?" they asked her. She answered, "They have taken my Lord away, and I do not know where they have put him!" [14]When she had said this, she turned around and saw Jesus standing there; but she did not know that it was Jesus. [15]"Woman, why are you crying?" Jesus asked her. "Who is it that you are looking for?" She thought he was the gardener, so she said to him, "If you took him away, sir, tell me where you have put him and I will go and get him." [16]Jesus said to her, "Mary!" She turned toward him and said in Hebrew, "Rabboni!" (This means "Teacher.") [17]"Do not hold on to me," Jesus told her, "because I have not yet gone back up to the Father. But go to my brothers and tell them for me, 'I go back up to him who is my Father and your Father, my God and your God.'"

[18]So Mary Magdalene told the disciples that she had seen the Lord, and that he had told her this.

The first thing the reader notices is that the one who is the first to believe is the "beloved disciple" (20:8), the one who rested his head on Jesus' chest at the Last Supper (see 13:23–25). The point John is making is that love gives one eyes to see what others cannot see. In 21:7, when the apostles are fishing and Jesus stands on the shore of the lake, it is the "beloved disciple" alone who recognizes him from a distance and informs Peter, "It is the Lord!" It is surely John's intention to present the "beloved disciple" as an example to be followed by his audience. The power of love is immense, and the "beloved disciple" exemplifies this power.

The "beloved disciple" believes Jesus has risen when he sees the linen burial cloths and "the cloth which had been around Jesus' head ... rolled up by itself" (20:5–8). Some explain that he believes because he reasons that if the body had been taken away by grave robbers, the robbers would certainly not have left the valuable linen cloths behind, nor would they have taken the time to roll up the head cloth. Others—more rightly, we think—explain that the "beloved disciple" believes because he sees that the position and the form of the cloths have preserved the rough outline of Jesus' body, and because the head cloth looks as if the one who had worn it had removed it and carefully rolled it up. Both explanations are equally possible and probable. We will never know, however, what was going through the mind of the "beloved disciple" as he came to his momentous conclusion!

The second thing the reader notices about John's account is that people who see Jesus after his resurrection have difficulty in recognizing him. Mary Magdalene thinks he is the gardener and recognizes him only when he speaks to her (20:14–16). Only the "beloved disciple," but not the others, recognizes Jesus from a distance (21:4–14). In Luke 24:13–35 the situation is the same. The two disciples on the road to Emmaus walk and talk with Jesus for some time before they recognize him in the breaking of the bread. The difficulties in recognizing Jesus prove that the disciples did not easily come to a belief in his resurrection from the dead.

More important than the difficulty in recognizing Jesus, however, is the reason for these difficulties. Jesus is changed. Following his resurrection, he is transformed in some way. It is because of this transformation that it is difficult to recognize him immediately. Significantly, Mary Magdalene does not recognize Jesus until she **hears** his voice. Jesus had said of the good shepherd that "the sheep hear his voice as he calls his own sheep by name" (10:3). Here Jesus calls Mary by name, and immediately she recognizes him! Mary Magdalene is an example for all but especially for those Jews on the fence at the end of the first century. When they hear Jesus, through the Spirit, calling them, they should respond as Mary does.

Another thing the reader should notice about Jesus' appearance to Mary Magdalene is the significance of Jesus' words: "Do not hold on to me, because I have not yet gone back up to the Father." When Jesus returns to the Father, he will send the Holy Spirit, and the Holy Spirit will be with Christians as another Jesus. If one reads what Jesus says about the Holy Spirit in 14:25–26 and 16:4b–15, one notes that Jesus' permanent presence is not by way of appearances now and then to select persons but by way of the gift of the Holy Spirit. It is fitting, therefore, that Jesus should tell Mary Magdalene not to hold on to him but rather to go and prepare his disciples for his coming and for his gift to them of the Spirit (see 20:19–23).

Lastly, John repeats his theme of "absence-presence" which he first brought up in the Last Supper discourse (see 13:33; 14:18; 28:29; 16:4b–15). He does so by means of Mary's repeated lament: "They have taken the Lord from the tomb, and I do not know where they have put him!" Christians, John is saying, will not always have the physical presence of Jesus, but they will have his presence in another way—through the Holy Spirit. It is the same for us today. Sometimes Jesus seems almost immediately present to us. At other times, he seems a million miles away. When we feel his absence, it is the time to pray: "Come, Holy Spirit!"

■ *Reflection*

Recall some personal "absence-presence" experiences of Jesus and their meaning in your following of Christ.

Sequence 21 (20:19—21:25) Jesus Appears to His Apostles

In the twenty-first and last sequence (20:19—21:25) of his Gospel, John continues to dramatize his inspired theological message. He arranges his material in his usual five-section format:

Parallel Structure of Sequence 21

Section one: Jesus **commissions** the apostles (20:19–23).

Section two: **Jesus' presence** is required for Thomas' conversion (20:24–29).

Section three: The purpose of the signs and of the book is to bring people to faith (20:30–31).

Section four: **Jesus' presence** is required for the catch of fish (21:1–14).

Section five: Jesus **commissions** Peter in a special way (21:15–25).

The sequence as a whole deals with the Church—its leadership under Peter and the other apostles, its faith, and the need for union with Jesus in order to carry out the missionary work of the Church.

Sequence 21 (20:19—21:25)

[19]It was late that Sunday evening, and the disciples were gathered together behind locked doors, because they were afraid of the Jews. Then Jesus came and stood among them. "Peace be with you," he said. [20]After saying this, he showed them his hands and his side. The disciples were filled with joy at seeing the Lord. [21]Then Jesus said to them again, "Peace be with you. As the Father sent me, so I send you." [22]He said this, and then he breathed on them and said, "Receive the Holy Spirit. [23]If you forgive men's sins, then they are forgiven; if you do not forgive them, then they are not forgiven."

[24]One of the disciples, Thomas (called the Twin), was not with them when Jesus came. [25]So the other disciples told him, "We saw the Lord!" Thomas said to them, "If I do not see the scars of the nails in his hands, and put my finger where the nails were, and my hand in his side, I will not believe." [26]A week later the disciples were together indoors again, and Thomas was with them. The doors were locked, but Jesus came and stood among them and said, "Peace be with you." [27]Then he said to Thomas, "Put your finger here, and look at my hands; then stretch out your hand and put it in my side. Stop your doubting and believe!" [28]Thomas answered him, "My Lord and my God!" [29]Jesus said to him, "Do you believe because you see me? How happy are those who believe without seeing me!"

[30]Jesus did many other mighty works in his disciples' presence which are not written down in this book. [31]These have been written that you may believe that Jesus is the Messiah, the Son

of God, and that through this faith you may have life in his name.

21 After this, Jesus showed himself once more to his disciples at Lake Tiberias. This is how he did it. ²Simon Peter, Thomas (called the Twin), Nathanael (the one from Cana in Galilee), the sons of Zebedee, and two other disciples of Jesus were all together. ³Simon Peter said to the others, "I am going fishing." "We will come with you," they told him. So they went and got into the boat; but all that night they did not catch a thing. ⁴As the sun was rising, Jesus stood at the water's edge, but the disciples did not know that it was Jesus. ⁵Then he said to them, "Young men, haven't you caught anything?" "Not a thing," they answered. ⁶He said to them, "Throw your net out on the right side of the boat, and you will find some." So they threw the net out, and could not pull it back in, because they had caught so many fish. ⁷The disciple whom Jesus loved said to Peter, "It is the Lord!" When Simon Peter heard that it was the Lord, he wrapped his outer garment around him (for he had taken his clothes off) and jumped into the water. ⁸The rest of the disciples came to shore in the boat, pulling the net full of fish. They were not very far from land, about a hundred yards away. ⁹When they stepped ashore they saw a charcoal fire there with fish and bread on it. ¹⁰Then Jesus said to them, "Bring some of the fish you have just caught." ¹¹Simon Peter went aboard and dragged the net ashore, full of big fish, a hundred and fifty-three in all; even though there were so many, still the net did not tear. ¹²Jesus said to them, "Come and eat." None of the disciples dared ask him, "Who are you?" because they knew it was the Lord. ¹³So Jesus went over, took the bread, and gave it to them;

he did the same with the fish. ¹⁴This, then, was the third time Jesus showed himself to the disciples after he was raised from death.

¹⁵After they had eaten, Jesus said to Simon Peter, "Simon, son of John, do you love me more than these?" "Yes, Lord," he answered, "you know that I love you." Jesus said to him, "Take care of my lambs." ¹⁶A second time Jesus said to him, "Simon, son of John, do you love me?" "Yes, Lord," he answered, "you know that I love you." Jesus said to him, "Take care of my sheep." ¹⁷A third time Jesus said, "Simon, son of John, do you love me?" Peter became sad because Jesus asked him the third time, "Do you love me?" and said to him "Lord, you know everything; you know that I love you!" Jesus said to him: "Take care of my sheep. ¹⁸I tell you the truth: when you were young you used to fasten your belt and go anywhere you wanted to; but when you are old you will stretch out your hands and someone else will tie them and take you where you don't want to go." (¹⁹In saying this Jesus was indicating the way in which Peter would die and bring glory to God.) Then Jesus said to him, "Follow me!" ²⁰Peter turned around and saw behind him that other disciple, whom Jesus loved— the one who had leaned close to Jesus at the meal and asked, "Lord, who is going to betray you?" ²¹When Peter saw him, he said to Jesus, "Lord, what about this man?" ²²Jesus answered him, "If I want him to live on until I come, what is that to you? Follow me!" ²³So a report spread among the followers of Jesus that this disciple would not die. But Jesus did not say that he would not die; he said, "If I want him to live on until I come, what is that to you?" ²⁴He is the disciple who spoke of these things, the one who also wrote them down; and

we know that what he said is true. [25]Now, there are many other things that Jesus did. If they were all written down one by one, I suppose that the whole world could not hold the books that would be written.

Section one (20:19–23) takes place on Easter Sunday evening. It opens with the disciples gathered behind locked doors for fear of the Jews. Jesus appears, and fear turns to joy! The joy comes from Jesus' presence and from the gift of peace promised by Jesus at the Last Supper (see 14:27 and 16:33).

Jesus commissions his apostles with the brief but dynamic declaration: "As the Father sent me, so I send you." He then breathes upon them and says: "Receive the Holy Spirit. If you forgive people their sins, they are forgiven, if you do not forgive them, they are not forgiven."

It is upon the words of John 20:23 and Matthew 16:19 that the Church bases its right and power to forgive sins in the sacrament of Reconciliation. If, however, we consider the words of John 20:23 in the light of his entire Gospel, we might see a deeper meaning in Jesus' words about forgiveness. For John's Jewish audience, the breath of God symbolizes the giving of power. We see these words then intimately related to the "work" of him whom the Baptist hailed as "the Lamb of God, who takes away the sin of the world" (1:29). We see Jesus letting his apostles share with him the authority to forgive or not forgive people's sins (20:23). Such an authority implies that the apostles are empowered by the breath of the Spirit to continue Jesus' work. Just as the Father sent Jesus to bring eternal life to all who believe him, so the apostles are now sent with the power to bring the world to belief in Jesus and so to eternal life.

Section two (20:24–29), in which John deals for the last time with his all-important theme of faith, dramatizes the well-known story of doubting Thomas. It is so vivid that most of us can even feel Thomas' embarrassment as Jesus takes him up on his statement and tells him to look at the scars on his hands and touch them and to put his hand in his side. However, John places this story in precisely this location to show his audience the kind of faith that is expected of all those who wish to be true members of the Church. It is a faith based not on miracles but on accepting the gift of the Holy Spirit and believing in Jesus through the testimony of others. Jesus says, "Do you believe because you see me? How happy are those who believe without seeing me!" To put across this point, as section three shows, is why John wrote his Gospel.

Section three (20:30–31) leaves no doubt in the reader's mind as to John's purpose in writing his Gospel. The Gospel is his testimony to Jesus, and miracles are part of that testimony. The "many other miracles" referred to in 20:30 are certainly the large number of miracles mentioned by Matthew, Mark, and Luke. However, in his Gospel, John uses only seven: the Cana miracle (2:1–12); the cure of the Roman official's son (4:46–54); the cure of the paralytic (5:1–18); the multiplication of the loaves (6:1–15); the cure of the man born blind (9:1–38); the raising of Lazarus (11:1–44); and the miraculous catch of fish (21:1–14). These seven are included in John's Gospel because they help to achieve his purpose in writing his Gospel: "that you may believe that Jesus is the Messiah, the Son of God, and that through your faith in him you may have life" (20:31). Having thus stated the purpose of his Gospel, John returns in sections four and five to the subject of the Church and its leaders. Quite fittingly he deals in a unique way with Peter, whom Jesus designates as the leader of the Church whose mission it is to bring the world to believe and thus to eternal life.

Section four (21:1–14) deals with Jesus' third and last appearance to his disciples. It takes place at the Lake of Galilee. Peter and six others have fished all night and caught nothing. At dawn, Jesus tells them to cast the net on the right side of the boat. The results are stupendous.

John's purpose in telling the story is both simple and profound. On the simple side, there is the basic message: "Without me you can do nothing!" All night long they catch nothing. When Jesus is with them, however, it is a different matter. The miraculous catch would remind the reader of Jesus' words: "A branch cannot bear fruit by itself; it can do so only if it remains in the vine" (15:4). For Christian missionaries, the message is clear. They are not alone. As long as they remain united with Jesus, he insures the success of their mission.

On the profound side, there is much symbolism. The fishing expedition represents the apostolic mission. The fish represent persons. And Jesus' words in 20:21 explain the apostles' mission: "As the Father sent me, so I send you." Jesus' work is to bring people to believe in him and thus receive eternal life. The work of the apostles is the same!

Also symbolic is the number of fish caught—153. Scholars agree the number has something to do with the universality of the Church. It was popularly believed in the first century that there were 153 different species of fish. If John is playing on this popular belief—though we are not sure he is—then the number 153 represents all the different nations of the world which will one day enter into Christ's Church.

Since only John mentions that the net was not torn (see 21:22 and compare with the version in Luke 5:1–11), scholars are inclined to see Johannine symbolism in this remark as well. The Church, this symbolism says, is one and remains one. It is another way of saying what Jesus says about his flock: "There are other sheep which belong to me that are not in this sheep pen. I must bring them, too; they will listen to my voice, and they will become one flock with one shepherd." (10:16).

Lastly, this scene is meant to throw the reader's mind back to Jesus walking on the water in sequence 11 (6:16–21). Both scenes take place at the lake. In both, the disciples do not recognize Jesus until he identifies himself. Such obvious parallels are designed to remind John's audience that the Church is the New Israel, that Jesus is the promised Savior, and that the apostles and their successors in union with Jesus continue the work of bringing the world to belief and to eternal life.

In considering the Church aspect of sequence 21, the reader should note that Peter is the one who leads the fishing trip. The significance of this detail becomes apparent in section five when Jesus singles out Peter from the other apostles and makes him vicar shepherd of the good shepherd's flock.

Section five (21:15–25) is the parallel to section one where Jesus commissioned the apostles as a group (20:19–23). In section five, however, Jesus, as the only true shepherd of the flock (see 10:1–21) commissions Peter in a special way by appointing him vicar of his Church. It is now up to Peter to lead, feed, and watch over Jesus' flock. This language is symbolic, of course, but the meaning is clear. Peter is commissioned to be the leader of Jesus' Church on earth. In Matthew 16:17–19, Jesus commissioned Peter as his vicar in equally symbolic terms. "I tell you Peter: you are a rock, and on this rock foundation I will build my church, and not even death will be able to overcome it."

Jesus' question, repeated three times, "Simon, son of John, do you love me more than these others do?" is frequently interpreted as Jesus' way of reminding Peter of his threefold denial of Jesus. This interpretation may be so, but as some scholars have pointed out, the threefold question and answer is not so much to indicate that Jesus doubts Peter but rather that Peter's love for Jesus is earnest. Before Jesus commissions Peter as vicar, he first demands to know if Peter loves him. This reading fits with the symbolism of the washing of the feet (13:1–32) and with what Jesus says about his "new commandment" (13:34–35). It also fits with what Jesus says about the Church's unity in love in and through the indwelling of the Father, the Son, and the Holy Spirit (17:20, 26).

John goes on in 21:18–19 to speak in symbolic terms about Peter's death. In 10:17, Jesus the good shepherd says of himself, "The Father loves me because I am willing to give up my life in order that I may receive it back again." When Jesus speaks about Peter's death, he is reminding Peter that if he, Peter, is to be truly his vicar, he must, like Jesus, be ready to lay down his life for his sheep. It is important to recall here that Peter did indeed follow Jesus to the cross. Jesus had said: "You cannot follow me now where I am going, but later you will follow me" (13:36). Thirty-four years later he followed Jesus. In the year 64 A.D., in Rome, Peter was crucified by the Roman emperor Nero!

Finally, it is of some significance that it is only after Peter has three times declared his love for Jesus that Jesus says to him, "follow me!" Only those who truly love Jesus can be effective shepherds of his flock.

In a Gospel that has many mysterious sayings, few are so mysterious as the last words of Jesus in John's Gospel and the last words of the evangelist himself.

Peter asks about the disciple whom Jesus loved, and Jesus responds, "If I want him to live until I come, what is that to you?" (21:23). The words "until I come" refer to Jesus' second coming in glory at the end of the world. One must ask, "Could Jesus have seriously considered letting the 'beloved disciple' live until the end of the world?" Most likely there was a rumor to this effect which the author here quashes with the explanation: "But Jesus did not say he would not die; he said, 'If I want him to live until I come, what is that to you?' " Many have tried to deduce from these words that the "beloved disciple" was dead by the time the Gospel was written. This deduction is not unlikely, but neither is it certain. The statement that follows in 21:24 does not say whether he is alive or dead. It does, however, attribute to him the writing of the Gospel. The question is: Is the author of the Gospel speaking about himself in 21:24, or are others speaking about him and recommending his Gospel? The greatest scholars have not been able to answer this question. Most think that verses 24–25 were added to the Gospel by a group of Christian elders who were giving their support to the theology of the author. This theory may be so, but it can never be proved that verses 24–25 are not the last words of the author himself. If they are, then the "beloved disciple" wrote the Gospel. However, no one has ever been able to identify the "beloved disciple." His name, whatever it was, is never given any place in the Gospel.

The "beloved disciple" is mentioned in 13:23; 18:15; 19:26; 20:3–9; and here in 21:20–25. He may even be the second of the two unnamed disciples mentioned in 1:35–39 and 21:2. If so, he has deliberately refused to identify himself. One may speculate concerning his identity, but that is all one can do. He decided to remain anonymous and has succeeded in so doing to the present day. He remains, naturally, a model for all who read his Gospel. Like him, the true Christian remains near to Jesus (13:23), stands beneath his cross (19:25), is closely attached to Mary his mother (19:26), and believes without seeing miracles (20:8). It is fitting that the Gospel ends with the words, "He is the disciple who spoke of these things, the one who also wrote them down; and we know that what he said is true!" (21:24).

■ *Reflection*
In depicting Mary's roles at Cana and on Calvary, what light does the Gospel of John shed on her unique role in the Church?

■ Discussion

1. Discuss: "Only those who truly love Jesus can be effective shepherds of his flock."

2. From the Gospel according to John, cite and discuss passages which illuminate the sacraments of Christian initiation (Baptism, Confirmation, Eucharist).

3. Find and discuss passages which shed light on the sacrament of Reconciliation.

4. In what sense may all grave sin be considered denial and rejection of Jesus?

5. Discuss the resurrection of the body as a principal truth of Christian faith.

6. What does the Gospel of John tell us about life after death?

■ Prayer and Meditation

"His royal power will continue to grow;
　　his kingdom will always be at peace.
He will rule as King David's successor,
　　basing his power on right and justice,
　　from now until the end of time."

Isaiah 9:7

"Then Jesus came and stood among them. 'Peace be with you,' he said. After saying this, he showed them his hands and his side. The disciples were filled with joy at seeing the Lord. Jesus said to them again, 'Peace be with you.' "

John 20:19b–21

Bibliography

R.E. Brown, *The Gospel of John*. Garden City, NY: Doubleday, 1966.

_____*The Community of the Beloved Disciple*. New York, NY—Ramsey, NJ— Toronto: Paulist, 1979.

_____"The Passion According to John: Chapters 18 and 19," *Worship* 49 (pp.126–134), March, 1975.

C.H. Dodd, *Historical Tradition in the Fourth Gospel*. London—New York, NY: Cambridge University Press, 1963.

R. Fortna, *The Gospel of Signs*. London—New York, NY: Cambridge University Press, 1970.

P.B. Harner, *The "I Am" of the Fourth Gospel*. Philadelphia, PA: Fortress Press, 1970.

R. Kysar, *The Fourth Evangelist and His Gospel*. Minneapolis, MN: Augsburg, 1975.

R.H. Lightfoot, *St. John's Gospel*. London—New York, NY: Oxford University Press, 1960.

B. Lindars, *The Gospel of John*. London: Oliphants, 1972.

J. Marsh, *Saint John*. Baltimore, MD: Penguin Books, 1968.

J.L. Martyn, *History and Theology in the Fourth Gospel*. Nashville, TN: Abingdon, 1979.

J. McPoin, *John*. Wilmington, DE: Michael Glazier, Inc., 1982.

J.F. O'Grady, "Recent Developments in Johannine Studies," *Biblical Theology Bulletin*, xii, pp. 54–58. April, 1982.

R. Schnackenburg, *The Gospel According to John*. New York, NY: Herder and Herder, 1968.

D.M. Smith, *The Composition and Order of the Fourth Gospel*. New Haven, CN: Yale University Press, 1965.

M.J. Taylor, ed., *A Companion to John*. New York, NY: Alba House, 1977.

H. Windisch, *The Spirit-Paraclete in the Fourth Gospel*. Philadelphia, PA: Fortress Press 1968.